Rusty Wallace
THE DECISION TO WIN

Rusty Wallace

THE DECISION TO WIN

By Bob Zeller with Rusty Wallace
Design by Tom Morgan

 DAVID BULL PUBLISHING

Acknowledgments

To assemble the story of Rusty Wallace, Rusty himself provided the big picture while his family and friends filled in the details. Don Miller, Rusty's longtime friend, adviser, and former business manager as well as the primary archivist of Rusty's career, opened his files, which contained dozens upon dozens of newspaper clips and photos.

Rusty's parents, Russ and Judy, provided dozens of priceless family photos as well as their own memories and insights. Rusty's wife, Patti, generously provided photos and checked the manuscript. Special thanks to Charlie Chase, who provided photos, Poor Boy Chassis Co. graphics, and stories, and to Kenny Wallace, who was a great interview as usual, but also helped identify many obscure photos.

National Speed Sport News and its editor, Chris Economaki, who often wrote about Rusty when he was a young, rising midwestern racer, were tremendously helpful in the preparation of this book. *NSSN* is one of the greatest papers of record for any sport. It's coverage allowed me to reconstruct Rusty's early career, race by race. Many thanks to Chris and his daughter, *NSSN* publisher Corinne Economaki, as well as Ron Lemasters, Jr., Mike Kerchner, and Cindy Blackwelder, for accommodating my research needs.

Thanks as well to Bobby Allison, Paul Andrews, Bill Brooks, Skylar Browning, John Childs, Walt Czarnecki, Dalmatian Black and White Photo Lab, Barry Dodson, John Erickson, Joyce Kearns, Dan Luginbuhl, Jimmy Makar, Bruce Martin, the late Gerald Martin, Mark Martin, Sally McMillan, Dick and Stella Paysor, Robin Pemberton, Roger Penske, Larry Phillips, Rocky Rhodes, Tom Roberts, Ken Schrader, Karen Smith, John Sonderegger, Marc Spiegel, Jeff Thousand, Dick Trickle, Mike Wallace, Sue Wallace, John and Justin Wiethop, Deb Williams, and Dave Wirz.

We recognize that some words, model names and designations mentioned in this book are the property of the trademark holder. We use them only for identification purposes.

First Printing

Library of Congress Cataloging-in-Publication Data
Zeller, Bob, 1952-
    Rusty Wallace / by Bob Zeller with Rusty Wallace ; foreword by Rusty Wallace.
            p.   cm.
        ISBN 1-893618-10-2. — ISBN 1-893618-09-9 (softcover)
        1. Automobile racing drivers — United States Biography.
    I. Wallace, Rusty, 1955 or 6- II. Title.
    GV1032.W35Z44   1999
    796.72' 092 —dc21
    [B]   99-40330
                                                                                CIP

ISBN 1-893618-09-9
Printed and bound in Hong Kong

Book and cover design: Tom Morgan, Blue Design, Portland, ME (www.bluedes.com)

10 9 8 7 6 5 4 3 2 1

David Bull Publishing
4250 E. Camelback Road, Suite K150
Phoenix, AZ 85018

602-852-9500
602-852-9503 (fax)

www.bullpublishing.com

Opposite: The furious action of a pit stop is evident in this image from the 1996 Goody's 500. This was one of many stops Rusty made on his way to his fifth and final victory of the 1996 season. (Nigel Kinrade)

Page 2: Rusty chats with Dick Trickle under the hood of Rusty's car before the Coca-Cola 300 at Lonesome Pine. Just visible in the background, a young Alan Kulwicki rubs his face. Rusty qualified on the outside of the first row, but Trickle won the race. (David Allio)

Page 6: Rusty won the 1988 Winston Cup race at Riverside—NASCAR's final appearance at the famed Southern California road course. The old track succumbed to suburban sprawl, but not before Rusty won his second straight there. The victory also gave him the Winston Cup points lead. (David Chobat)

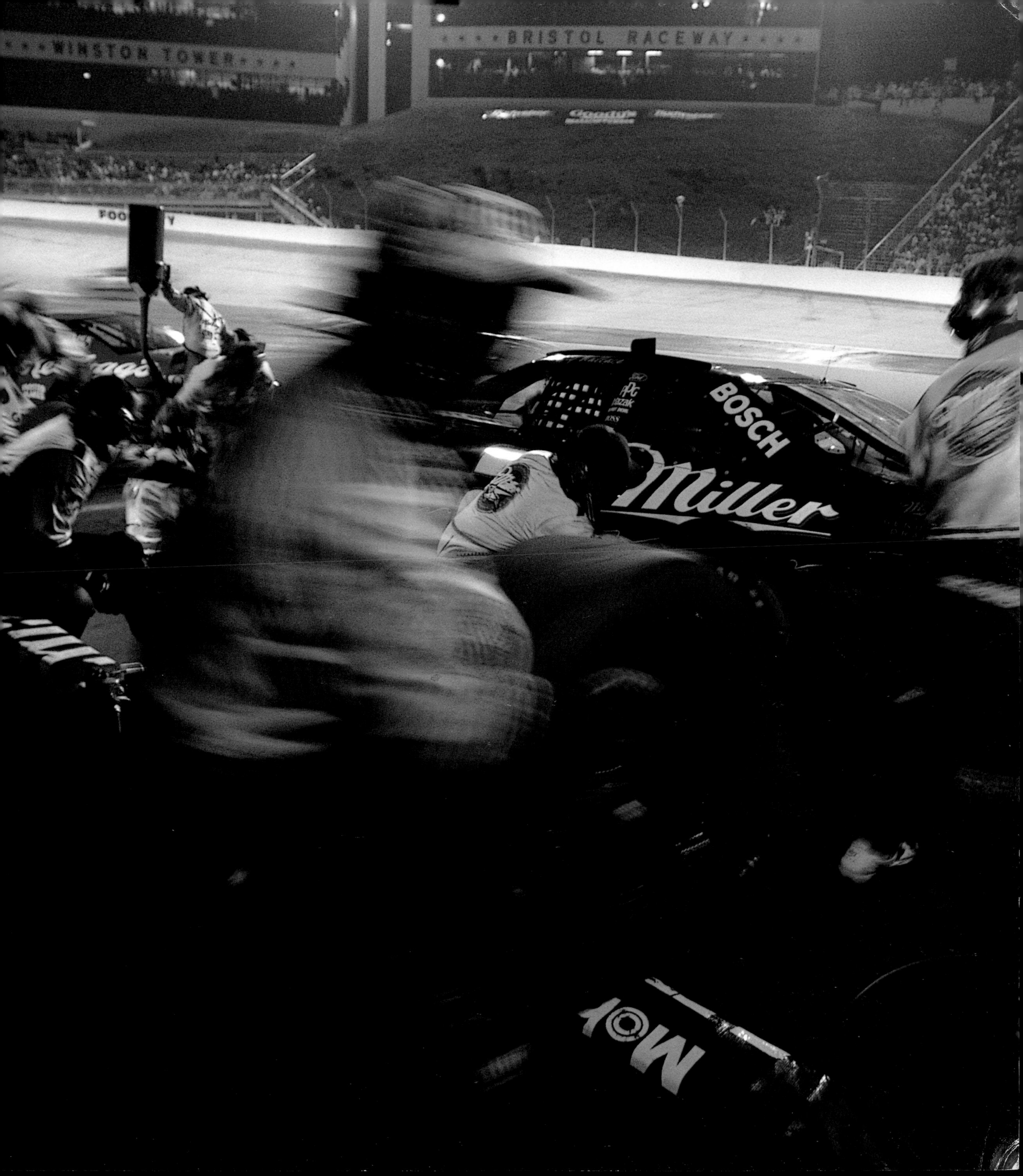
WINSTON TOWER
BRISTOL RACEWAY
BOSCH
Miller

Contents

1. A Court Order to Race 10

2. Stock Cars in a Stick-and-Ball Town 24

3. Poor Boy Chassis Company 34

4. The Evil Gang Hits the Road 46

5. Learning from a Legend 58

6. Challenging A.J. Foyt 70

7. A Face Full of Mud 84

8. A Championship and Another Chance 96

9. Becoming a Contender 108

10. Winning the Championship on a Wing and a Prayer 122

11. Year of Triumph, Year of Trauma 134

12. A Racer's Life 146

Foreword

From the time I was ten years old I was determined to be a race-car driver. My dad was a racer, and as I worked on his car at home and watched him race from the stands I knew that was what I wanted to do with my life—get in a race car and drive it as hard and fast as it could go. My whole family was that way.

I started as soon as I could, driving my first race right after my sixteenth birthday. From the beginning I had to finance my racing pretty much on my own by working part-time jobs. Later, with the help of some friends, I started my own company to pay for my racing. I made racing my job. I had a lot of successes as well as my share of failures. When I look back at my early years it's hard to believe all of the hardships and struggles that we went through to race. You'll read many of those stories in this book.

I wanted to do this book so people would know where I came from, and how I got to where I am today. Not a lot of people know about my early racing career in the ASA and USAC, or how I got started with Don Miller and Roger Penske. Bob Zeller has done an amazing job of bringing to life the stories from my early career.

If I learned one thing along the way it's the power of persistence. If you absolutely positively commit to do something, then you're going to do it and you're probably going to do it well. I've succeeded at the highest levels of my sport because I was bound and determined to do it. But we also never lost sight of having a little fun along the way.

Maybe my story will inspire you a little bit, too, and help you find within yourself the drive it takes to make the decision to win, no matter what you're involved in.

Rusty Wallace
Mooresville, July 1999

Opposite: Under a clearing Arizona sky, Rusty leads Ken Schrader and Bill Elliott into the first turn at Phoenix International Raceway during the rain-shortened Dura-Lube 500. Rusty was ahead when the event was stopped after 257 laps. It was his only victory in 1998 and broke a fifty-nine-race nonwinning streak. (Nigel Kinrade)

"We, Russ Wallace and Judy Wallace, parents of Rusty Wallace, give our concent [*sic*] for Rusty to participate in the racing program at Lake Hill Speedway."

The idea that Rusty was a born racer is strengthened by this photograph of him at about age one, sitting confidently and happily behind the wheel of a model of a brand-new 1957 Chevrolet Corvette. (Wallace collection)

Opposite: Wearing a cotton shirt and an open-faced helmet, Rusty raced for the first time at sixteen years and six days on August 20, 1972, at Lake Hill Speedway in Valley Park, Missouri. His '69 Chevelle is painted in gray primer. His number, 66, which is taped to the door with duct tape, is taken from his father's traditional number, 6. (Wallace collection)

On Monday, August 14, 1972, Judy Wallace and her oldest son, Russell William Wallace Jr., appeared in the courtroom of Judge Robert G. J. Hoester in the juvenile court of the county of St. Louis, Missouri, and made an unusual request. She asked the court to allow her sixteen-year-old son to go stock car racing.

"Let the record show that Mr. and Mrs. Russell Wallace, parents of Russell William Wallace (Jr.), appeared in open court and acknowledged that they consented to their son, Russell William, sixteen years of age, born August 14, 1956, to participate in racing automobiles at the Lake Hill Speed Way in the County of St. Louis, State of Missouri, and attached to this copy of this order is the signed release signed in open Court on this 14th day of August, 1972. Said proceedings and consent freely given in open Court."

Hoester looked at the court document he was being asked to sign. He smiled. He asked Rusty if he knew the dangers of what he was getting into.

"Yes," Rusty said.

The judge looked at the release. It said, "We, Russ Wallace and Judy Wallace, parents of Rusty Wallace, give our concent [*sic*] for Rusty to participate in the racing program at Lake Hill Speedway."

It surely was one of the simplest matters on the judge's docket that day. Although a sixteen-year-old could get a driver's license in Missouri, you had to be eighteen to race at Lake Hill Speedway unless you obtained a court order and your parents signed a release. Hoester signed several copies of the order, and the Wallaces were on their way.

Six days later, on the evening of Sunday, August 20, Rusty Wallace made his racing debut. Today it seems like ancient history to him. But in 1972, it was a long-awaited event for not only Rusty, but his entire family.

IN THE MATTER

OF

IN THE

JUVENILE COURT

County of St. Louis Missouri

Juvenile No._____

RUSSELL WILLIAM WALLACE
a minor.

August 14_____, 19_72_

Let the record show that Mr. and Mrs. Russell Wallace,

parents of Russell William Wallace, appeared in open Court and

acknowledged that they consented to their son, Russell William,

sixteen years of age, born August 14, 1956, to participate in

racing automobiles at the Lake Hill Speed Way in the County of

St. Louis, State of Missouri, and attached to this copy of this

order is the signed release signed in open Court on this 14th

day of August, 1972. Said proceedings and consent freely given

in open Court.

ROBERT G. J. HOESTER   Judge

This is the court order that allowed Rusty to race at age sixteen at Lake Hill Speedway. Judy Wallace got several copies in case Rusty went to other tracks. Ken Schrader obtained a similar court order to race at sixteen, as did Rusty's younger brother, Mike. (Wallace collection)

Opposite: Just six days after he turned sixteen, Rusty was racing at Lake Hill Speedway. (Wallace collection)

Before his debut, he and his father had come to the track early several times. "He let me practice with the car," Rusty says. "So I was comfortable when it came time for my first race."

Lake Hill Speedway was a one-third-mile paved oval sandwiched between two railroad tracks in the St. Louis suburb of Valley Park. The racers entered the infield through a narrow tunnel under one set of train tracks. After they unloaded and started working on their cars, they had to watch their backs for out-of-control racers spinning off the track.

"In my first race, I passed a bunch of cars, took the lead, and won the thing," Rusty says. "It was wild. I remember running the race, and then all of this jubilation, and then we raced in the feature—and ran out of gas. I think I lasted about ten laps. Won my first damn race and was so excited, I forgot to put gas in the car."

Russ Wallace won the late-model feature that night, as he often did that season. Four

Rusty won his first race at Lake Hill Speedway. Here he poses with the checkered flag on the frontstretch. In the euphoria of winning he forgot to put more gas in his car and ran out in the feature race. (Wallace collection)

days later, when the weekly edition of *National Speed Sport News* came off the presses, a tiny, three-paragraph story on page twelve carried the headline: "Wallace Wins at Lake Hill." Rusty's victory also was mentioned in the venerable racing newspaper: "Heat winners were [Butch] Cooley, Jerry Bieke, [Ed] Domijan, and 16-year-old Rusty Wallace, competing in his very first race." (As Rusty remembers it, his victory came in a semifeature race).

As a teenager, Judy Buckles was one of the regulars at the local hangout, the Kwikway Diner at the corner of Morgan Ford Road and Arsenal Street in St. Louis. Here Judy (left) posed with a waitress at the diner. (Wallace collection)

Rusty was just days old in this snapshot of the new family taken in the kitchen of Russ and Judy's home on South Broadway Street in St. Louis. This image was pasted in a booklet called "My Personal Record Since Birth," which Judy compiled during the first two years of Rusty's life. (Wallace collection)

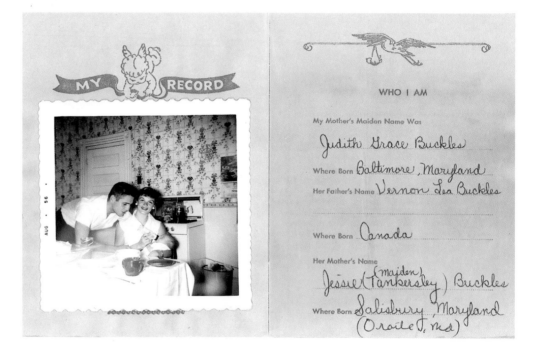

MY RECORD

AUG · 56

WHO I AM

My Mother's Maiden Name Was
Judith Grace Buckles
Where Born Baltimore, Maryland
Her Father's Name Vernon Lea Buckles

Where Born Canada

Her Mother's Name
Jessie (Tankersley) Buckles
(maiden)
Where Born Salisbury, Maryland
(Oriole, Md)

Three weeks after his first outing, Rusty finished second in a feature race to family friend Jerry Sifford. And on September 17, 1972, in a special 100-lap race at Lake Hill, Sifford prevailed over Russ Wallace after a furious battle. Ken Schrader, who also got his start at Lake Hill Speedway, finished third. Rusty was fourth. But his performance again was mentioned in *National Speed Sport News*, which reported that Rusty "astounded the fans with racing prowess beyond his years."

Rusty spent the next three seasons cutting his teeth at Lake Hill Speedway, but the driver to beat at the tiny paved oval was his father, Russ. Today Rusty sometimes hears other second-generation drivers like Dale Earnhardt talk about their fathers. "I just wish there were some way my dad could have competed against those guys," he says. "He probably would have given them a good whipping."

In Russ Wallace's prime, he dominated the races not only at the paved track at Lake Hill, but at a dirt track—Tri City Speedway—just across the Mississippi River in Granite City, Illinois. But he raced only as a hobby. He always had a full-time job, other part-time jobs, and side work as well, repairing cars. Some of the work, such as delivering newspapers, kept his sons busy, too, which was fine with Russ. It kept the family together and kept the boys out of trouble.

Russell William Wallace Sr. was the son of a St. Louis city bus driver named William Russell Wallace and his wife, Marie George Wallace. In his spare time, Russ's father sold vacuum cleaners. Later he opened his own small vacuum cleaner store and passed it on to his son, Gary. Russ eventually joined his brother there. Rusty and his brothers, Mike and Kenny, all worked at the vacuum store, too, although they hated every minute of it.

Rusty's mother, Judith Grace Buckles Wallace, was the fiery, redheaded daughter of Vernon Lea and Jessie Tankersley Buckles. Her father, a native of Canada, played semi-pro hockey for the Baltimore Orioles hockey team and later worked as a referee and announcer. He became a salesman for various companies and moved his family to St. Louis in 1949, when Judy was twelve.

Russ Wallace and Judy Buckles met in 1953 at the local hangout—the Kwikway Diner.

"My dad looked like Marlon Brando," Rusty says. "He wore a black leather jacket and boots and rode a stripped-down Harley—the whole deal."

"He was different," says Judy. "A lot of the girls were afraid of him. He wasn't a fighter-type guy. But he had the look that intimidated. Nobody ever challenged him or messed with him."

Judy, full of Irish blood, wasn't intimidated by anything. She could see past Russ's image. And she saw the qualities she wanted in a man. "I knew at seventeen years old that I would

Rusty was about two years old when this photograph of Russ and Judy was taken at Lake of the Ozarks in southwest Missouri. Russ was twenty-four; Judy was twenty-one. (Wallace collection)

"My dad looked like Marlon Brando," Rusty says. "He wore a black leather jacket and boots and rode a stripped-down Harley—the whole deal."

never starve to death with him," she says. "He had so much energy. He worked hard. He worked side jobs and sold cars on the side. He'd go buy an old truck and fix it up and sell it. He did mechanical work at night. He wanted the best of everything. And he was a problem solver. There was never a problem he wouldn't try to figure out."

Russ was his own man then and remains so now. He didn't need anyone telling him how to live his life. "I was always hooked on cars and motorized sports," he says. "When I went to high school, they told me I'd have to take woodworking. I wanted to take auto mechanics. I said, 'Not me. Good-bye.' I quit and went to work. Jobs were plentiful then. We were never without work. Never ever. If you lost a job at twelve o'clock, you had another one at one o'clock."

The young couple was already into racing when they married on September 3, 1955. Russ had worked for a man named Orville Herzog, who fielded a car when organized stock car racing started in St. Louis with the opening of Lake Hill Speedway in the early 1950s. Ken Schrader's father, Bill, also raced at Lake Hill from the beginning.

Russ started as a pit boy for Herzog. In 1953, when he was eighteen, he was so bitten by the racing bug, he seriously considered quitting his better-paying job in the service department at Sears Roebuck & Co. and taking three lesser jobs to make the same money because he couldn't get off Fridays to go to the races.

Outside the Wallaces' Spanish Lake home in 1960, Judy stands by the family toy—a red Chevrolet Impala convertible. A portion of the Wallace home is visible on the left side of the image. (Wallace collection)

One night in 1954, Herzog couldn't make it to the track, so he told Russ to race his car. Russ held his own against Bill Schrader and other older drivers. And he loved it.

After Russ married Judy, he built his own race car. His first victory was a forty-lap feature on a Friday night in 1956 at Belle-Clair Speedway, a quarter-mile track in Belleville, Illinois. But Rusty was born that same year, and by the time Mike was born in 1959, Russ had stopped racing. There were too many other demands on his time. It was expensive. And he was tired of juggling all of the responsibilities.

At birth, Rusty weighed in at a healthy 8 pounds and 4 ounces. Almost immediately, he began to exhibit some of his most distinctive personality traits. At three months, Judy wrote, "He rolls over now every time I lay him on his stomach. He is very strong now and talks and laughs all the time." At six months, he started crawling. "Once Rusty got started, he never stops," she wrote. "He's a very apt baby and learns very fast. Also a strong one."

In the spring of 1956, Russ Wallace stood next to the first race car he ever built, a 1937 Ford. He also raced it, although the name "Bob Mueller" appears on the door. "Bob was going to drive it but never did," Russ says. (Wallace collection)

At four months old, Rusty crawled on his father's stomach on the kitchen floor of their St. Louis home. He began teething two months later and at a year old weighed twenty-five pounds. (Wallace collection)

The Wallaces moved to the suburban neighborhood of Spanish Lake shortly before this photograph was taken. Here, three-and-a-half-year-old Rusty sits on his tricycle with his brother Mike, who was fifteen months old. (Wallace collection)

Kenny, the youngest of Russ and Judy's three sons, was born in 1963, the same year the family moved from St. Louis to Rolla, a small Missouri college town on Interstate 44 about 100 miles southwest of St. Louis. Russ and Judy thought Rolla would be a nice place to raise their sons. It also presented a business opportunity.

Russ's primary job beginning in 1958 had been delivering newspapers—the *St. Louis Globe-Democrat* and the *Post-Dispatch*. In St. Louis, people bought and owned their own routes, and delivering newspapers was their primary job. Routes were far less expensive in Rolla. Russ not only delivered the *Post-Dispatch* in Rolla, he owned a couple of service stations and ran a small taxi service. He also owned a house for engineering students near the University of Missouri–Rolla.

Once, when Rusty was ten or eleven years old, he was hanging out with the engineering students while they were making a float for the city's St. Patrick's Day parade. Rusty stayed up most of the night making his own float—a little Snoopy car. And when the students' float came along in the parade, Rusty was right behind, covered in green, driving his Snoopy car.

Around that time, racing came to Rolla when a small quarter-mile asphalt track known as Charlea Speedway opened with Friday night stock car races. Russ had been bowling on Friday nights. He quit bowling, purchased a 1955 Chevrolet with a leaf-spring rear suspension and eight-lug rear wheels, put a home-built roll cage in it, and went racing.

Judy and her three sons watched from the grandstand. "As soon as the race was over, we'd fly down the front straightaway and run into the pit area," Rusty recalls. "Dad and all his buddies would be getting together. And we'd all go down to the all-night restaurant by the freeway and have breakfast at three o'clock in the morning. The scene probably hasn't changed much. It's grassroots racing."

Rusty loved hanging around the garage while his dad was working on the race car. He loved anything mechanical.

"In Rolla, we would roll the newspapers in our garage before we delivered them," Judy says. "Usually we had the radio blaring. One time the radio quit. Well, Rusty was about eight or nine then. He said, 'I'll fix it.' He didn't want to roll papers anyway. By gosh, he had every part of that radio out on the workbench. He put it back together again and it worked."

A toy gun, a wagon, a dump truck, a toy race car, and some new shirts are part of the haul on Christmas Day 1961 as Rusty, four, and Mike, going on two, pose in front of the Wallaces' Christmas tree. (Wallace collection)

Another August summer in St. Louis in the 1960s brought another birthday party for Rusty. This is Rusty's fifth birthday celebration in the backyard of the Wallaces' Spanish Lake home on August 14, 1961. (Wallace collection)

"We were always coming and going. I can't ever remember us sitting down and having what they call dinner. It was always bologna and cheese sandwiches and out the door."

A young Russ and Judy Wallace pose with their sons outside their Spanish Lake home around 1961. Russ was not actively racing at this time. He resumed racing in the late 1960s. (Wallace collection)

Says Rusty: "I was always taking stuff apart and putting it back together. I'll go out to the garage today, and my youngest son, Stephen, will have his go-cart in pieces all over the place, and he'll say, 'I'm doing this,' and 'I'm doing that.' He reminds me of me."

Aside from their passion for racing, the Wallaces were a typical family. They had a couple of German shepherds, then a poodle named Pixie that had three puppies. They took summer trips to places like Frontier City and Six Flags over Missouri. Judy bought a Super 8 home movie camera and took movies that look like everyone else's home movies, with women wearing beehive hairdos, men in bell-bottom slacks, and everyone mugging for the camera when it panned their way.

No one in the family made more faces than Kenny. He was a natural ham. Kenny was always talking at 100 MPH and bouncing off the walls. One movie clip shows Kenny at about five years old, sitting in the middle of the living room floor with an open-face helmet on his head, running two Hot Wheels cars along a piece of banked, curved track, tapping the front bumper of one into the back bumper of the other.

Kenny used to visit the announcing booth at Lake Hill Speedway before the races started and pretend to be the track announcer, jabbering away at a mile a minute. One night, after a race at Ft. Leonard Wood, Missouri, Russ and Judy visited a place called Lou's Lounge and, of course, took the kids with them. While the parents were enjoying themselves, Kenny was running around the back of the lounge. "They had dancing girls in there, and Kenny was talking to every one of them," recalls Judy. Says Russ: "We're up front dancing, and Kenny is back at the pool tables, keeping the soldiers in stitches, just talking their butts off."

When the country singer Marty Robbins came to Springfield, Missouri, for a short-track race, Kenny walked right up to him and said, "Hello, Mr. Robbins. Will you sing 'El Paso' for me?" Kenny says today, "I thought because he was a singer, he'd just start singing right away."

Mike always did well at Fox Senior High School. He enrolled in a special program that offered technical classes at nearby Jefferson College. He won second prize in a class contest for building a scale model of a 5,000-square-foot luxury home using the original blueprints. "It was quite a project," Mike says. "I still don't know why I didn't win."

But like the rest of the family, Mike devoted most of his time to racing. "We were kind of a unique family," Mike says. "Racing is what we did. We didn't know there were a lot of other things in life to be doing."

"Our family was fun to grow up in," says Kenny. "We were always coming and going. The Wallace family was never one to sit down and have a nice meal at the dinner table. I can't ever remember us sitting down and having what they call dinner. It was always bologna and cheese sandwiches and out the door."

In 1969, the Wallaces left Rolla, moved back to St. Louis, and eventually settled in the south St. Louis suburb of Arnold in a ranch-style house on the side of a hill with a detached two-bay garage. Business hadn't been as good in Rolla as Russ had hoped. The family had gotten low on money. Russ's taxi drivers kept cheating him on fares. And the student house hadn't been the best income producer, either. It was vacant three months of the year. The cost of Russ's racing didn't help.

In June 1968, when Rusty was eleven, the Wallaces visited friends in Mineral Wells, Texas, and Rusty had the opportunity to sit in a U.S. Army helicopter at the helicopter training base at Fort Wolters. The base has since been closed and is now an industrial park. (Wallace collection)

One of Russ's friends had been pleading with him to take over the service department of his car dealership in St. Louis. Finally Russ agreed. Three years later, in 1972, he went into the family business at the OK Vacuum shop in Kirkwood.

Russ continued to race after the move back to St. Louis. And he was getting better and better every year. He still went to Rolla and raced nearly every weekend, almost always with the whole family in tow. A fast new half-mile paved oval—the Rolla Speedway—had opened and was attracting some big-name drivers in the region.

Often several racing families, including the Schraders, would drive down to Rolla and rent rooms at the Holiday Inn. The kids would play in the pool all afternoon, doing flips off the diving board or chicken fighting in the water. Usually it was Rusty and Mike versus Ken Schrader and Kenny.

Russ enjoyed returning to Rolla to race because the competition was tougher there. He had to battle seasoned short-track drivers like Larry Phillips, Terry Brumley, and Terry Bivins. Russ didn't win every week as he usually did at Lake Hill Speedway. His goal at Rolla was to make $250 to cover expenses, which he did if he finished third in the feature.

Russ was well liked among his fellow competitors, and one of the most important friendships he made was with Phillips. A legend in short-track stock car racing, Phillips is a five-time NASCAR Winston Racing series national champion. No other driver has won more than once. And he didn't begin winning those titles until 1989. But even in the early 1970s, Phillips was well known at tracks throughout the Midwest and South.

Phillips was a full-time racer. And when Phillips started building and selling race cars in his shop in Springfield, Missouri, Russ was among the first to buy one. It was one of the best moves Russ ever made. He won dozens of races in his Phillips-built car.

Left: A portrait of Rusty at twelve. (Wallace collection)

21

"...we rode in that salt mine all day long. It just tore the hell out of the motorcycles. They would be rusted and the chains would dry out."

When this school portrait of Rusty at fifteen was made in 1971, he was already an accomplished race car fabricator and mechanic and a regular pit crew member for his father. One year later, he would begin driving himself. (Wallace collection)

This photo taken from a Wallace family home movie shows Rusty on his Czechoslovakian-made CZ motorcycle before a motocross race at Riverdale. The 360 cc two-stroke bike was enormously powerful. (Wallace collection)

Not too many years later, Rusty followed in his father's footsteps, achieving some of his greatest early success driving a chassis built by Phillips.

But before Rusty began racing stock cars, he rode motorcycles. He raced for several years and won four out of seven American Motorcycle Association–sanctioned local motocross events. But Rusty never considered himself that good at it. And he still enjoyed working on cars more than motorcycles.

Like everything else in the Wallace household, the motocross races were family affairs. While Rusty and Mike were riding their motorcycles, Kenny would fly around on a three-wheeled all-terrain cycle. Even Judy would sometimes take a bike for a spin.

"We had a lot of fun riding," Rusty recalls. "Kenny Schrader was always finding great places to ride. He took us to a salt mine at Bonne Terre [about 50 miles south of St. Louis] and we rode in that salt mine all day long. It just tore the hell out of the motorcycles. They would be rusted and the chains would dry out. But there were miles and miles of trails. I had a 100cc Hodaka cycle and later I had a 360cc motorcycle called a CZ. It was made in Czechoslovakia, and it was a real bad-ass piece of machinery with tons of horsepower."

Wrecks and injuries were considered part of the territory. Once Rusty proudly displayed a nasty foot wound while his mother was filming with her movie camera. Russ had two bad crashes. In addition to the wreck that broke his leg in 1971, Russ had a crash at Rolla that was so hard, the impact popped the centers out of two of the wheels. He broke no bones but spent two days in the hospital recovering from the effects of the impact.

Rusty's worst crash as a teenager happened in the first corner of the first lap of a motocross race. "All I can remember is fifty bikes running over top of me," he says. "I mean, I got run over big-time bad. I woke up in the ambulance on the way to the hospital. I remember looking up and somebody said, 'You were the first one in the corner, and you laid it down, and boy, the whole damn field went right over top of you.'"

Rusty was bruised, battered, and cut. And he had a big indentation in his helmet. "So I went to the shop and put big old hunks of fiberglass over it and layered it and sanded it down. Then I spray painted that sucker and went back out and used it again," he says. "It never bothered me at all to crash back then. I think about it a lot more nowadays—about ways to survive crashes. I put all sorts of trick stuff in cars. Back then it was get in and go."

With buried tires serving as the berm at Missouri's tiny Fort Leonard Wood Speedway, Russ Wallace hugs the bottom of the groove in his 1955 Chevy. A friend, Danny Blades, was the owner of Blade's Shoe Shack in Rolla, as well as the car, although Russ maintained it. This photograph was taken in the spring of 1967. (Wallace collection)

"I knew a lot about race cars before I ever drove one," Rusty says. "I was helping my dad prepare his car all the time."

Racing through a turn at Lake Hill Speedway, Rusty has the same look of concentration as his father as he checks his mirror for traffic. Russ usually won their personal battles on the track during Rusty's first years of racing. (Wallace collection)

Opposite: Russ Wallace was one of the top drivers at Lake Hill Speedway when this photo was taken around 1973. (Wallace collection)

During the summer of 1972, as Rusty's sixteenth birthday approached, the Wallace family was immersed in racing. All three boys were working on their father's car. Kenny, only eight, was mostly just hanging around. But Mike, at thirteen, was handling harder tasks. And Rusty, at fifteen, was a seasoned race car mechanic, with experience working on not only his father's cars, but cars owned by his father's friends, such as Jerry Sifford, one of the best Lake Hill racers.

"I knew a lot about race cars before I ever drove one," Rusty says. "I was helping my dad prepare his car all the time." And Russ was winning more than ever. In May of 1972, he went on a rampage, winning five consecutive feature races at Lake Hill before Larry Phillips came to town in mid-June and ended the streak. Russ promptly started another one. On July 9, 1972, he set a new Lake Hill track record of 15.71 seconds and won the twenty-five-lap feature. On July 30, he lowered the track record to 15.4 seconds and won a seventy-five-lap feature, even though he spun on the twenty-third lap. He won again on August 6. Just two days before Rusty's sixteenth birthday, Russ won a fifty-lap feature at Rolla. Then, the night before Rusty's trip to the courthouse, Russ chased a driver named Paul Lawson for twenty-four laps in the Sunday night feature at Lake Hill, then passed him on the last lap. Russ easily won the 1972 late-model championship at Lake Hill.

Behind the wheel, Russ was aggressive but smooth. "When I got behind you, if you weren't going, I'd tap you once. Then I'd tap you a second time. The third time, I moved you," Russ says. Reel after reel of Wallace home movie film shows Russ slicing through packs of cars at Lake Hill, Charlea, and other small tracks. He had a special knack for passing on the outside. It was less crowded up there, and safer.

But Russ's success made him unpopular. "At first the fans liked us," recalls Kenny, who watched from the grandstand with his mother and her racing friends. "Then we won so much, they hated us."

John Sonderegger, who has written about motorsports for the *St. Louis Post-Dispatch* for more than twenty-five years, recalls: "Old Lake Hill Speedway was a third-mile asphalt track down in the boonies. It was a good place to go, except for the mosquitoes. When I first went there, I thought I was back in 1958 with the style of dress and the sideburns. Old Russ, he was top dog there. And everybody would boo him. They hated him.

"He'd pull in there with his race car, and Rusty would be sitting on the back of the truck, grinning like a rooster. People would be screaming at them. Judy, she was a hellcat. She'd prance around in the grandstands, screaming back at people. And there would be fights practically every week."

Russ was popular among his fellow racers. He rarely had trouble with anyone in the infield, although he does remember tearing the toupee off the head of a man who got in his face. But it was not so cordial in the grandstands. Judy always came armed with a big, heavy purse.

"I'll never forget the time I heard a guy scream: 'Crash, Russ Wallace! I hope you burn to death!'" says Kenny. "And my mom went after him. She'd beat your ass. She's Irish, and she grew up on the streets of Baltimore. She and her sister, my Aunt Millie, lived above some bars and grew up pretty rough."

Says Judy: "I just couldn't imagine that anyone would come right up in front of me, look me right in the face, call one of my kids or my husband a bad name, and expect me to stand there and not do anything. Then this guy says, 'I hope he burns to death.' I went ballistic. I'm not proud of that. But I thought they were rude sometimes, and I wanted them to remember it. So they learned not to sit too close to me."

"The word got out," says Russ. "Don't mess with Mama. And I tell you what, a man 6-foot-three; she'd challenge him to his face. One night during intermission, some guy came out of the grandstand and said, 'You better go up there and take care of your old lady.' I said, 'She can handle herself. She's on her own.'"

During Rusty's first full season in 1973, he and his father raced together at Lake Hill, driving a pair of red 1969 Chevelles. Russ drove Number 6. Rusty drove Number 66 and was rookie of the year. On a typical night, both would win a heat. Or Russ would win the trophy dash and Rusty would win the semifeature, or vice versa. On July 22, they finished one-two in a feature race.

In 1974, Russ and Rusty continued to trade victories at Lake Hill. Russ was now in a 1972 Camaro; Rusty was still driving the '69 Chevelle. Russ won the track championship and Rusty was second. Ken Schrader was sixth.

By then, Schrader and Rusty had developed a fierce rivalry. Schrader was a year older. One night, according to Kenny Wallace, Schrader and Rusty were slamming into each other on the track. Somehow Rusty got the better of him. When Schrader came back in the pits, his car was wrecked and smoking. His dad, Bill, bent down to the window and said, "You go back out there and get that boy." And he did.

That may have been the same night Schrader best remembers. He said he and Rusty expended so much effort smashing and crashing each other, they were both threatened with a suspension and given $100 fines. That stung plenty. A hundred dollars was a fortune to a couple of teenaged racers.

"They had to pull me out of the car," Rusty recalls. "I remember I was so mad, I pulled off that racetrack and went running through the pits wide open, aiming for his pit crew guys, because they were a bunch of jerks, too. I was going to run over all of them."

Rusty usually managed to avoid trouble, even in the face of hostile fans. "There was some rough stuff going on around me, but I didn't get into fights," he says. "I was always

Rusty, Russ, and Mike pose in front of Russ's race car at the Granite City, Illinois, dirt track during the 1972 season. By this time, all three of the Wallace brothers were active in maintaining and preparing the car. (Wallace collection)

hanging around all the top guys, whether it was Pete Hamilton or Bobby Allison or Larry Phillips."

Rusty graduated from Fox Senior High School in 1974, but only after attending summer school. He had done well in elementary school, but as the focus of his life turned toward racing, school became, as Rusty says, "just a big pain in the butt."

"My mind was always on the race car," Rusty says. "My mind was always somewhere else. The day would take forever in school. I wanted to be back in the garage at home, working on a race car."

He knew math well enough—when it came to calculating race car measurements. But in school, math went in one ear and out the other. College? "I thought, 'Why would you want to spend four years in college when you could be racing?'" says Rusty. "But my kids are not like that at all. They love school. My oldest son, Greg, is an outstanding student. My daughter, Katie, would go to school from eight in the morning until eight at night if she could. My little guy, Stephen, never complains. Mike did well in school, but Kenny was just like me. Sometimes we'd have trouble staying awake in class because we'd stayed up so late the night before working on the race car."

Says Kenny: "You can talk all you want about reality and morality and what's right and what's wrong, but we were focused. We didn't give a damn about math or English or social studies. We were going to race, and that's the way it was. We were smart; we just didn't put it in school. We knew we had to go, but we hated it. We just couldn't imagine racing not being our entire life."

As with his racing career, Rusty had generous help when it came to schoolwork. It came from his girlfriend and future wife, Patti Hall, who used to hang around Lake Hill with her father, Ed, who helped Russ in the pits. Patti did Rusty's homework, and he finally graduated.

The 1975 season opened with a bang at Lake Hill Speedway. A driver named Allen Potter literally flew out of the track and crashed so spectacularly, a photograph of the wreck was published on the front page of *National Speed Sport News* with the headline: "Into the Wild Blue Yonder." The image shows Potter's '69 Chevelle about 30 feet in the air outside the first and second turns at the moment it splintered a light pole. Judy was in the grandstand, and she captured the crash with her home movie camera as she filmed her husband. It was an incredible crash for a bull ring like Lake Hill and a reminder that danger always lurks in racing, no matter how small the track.

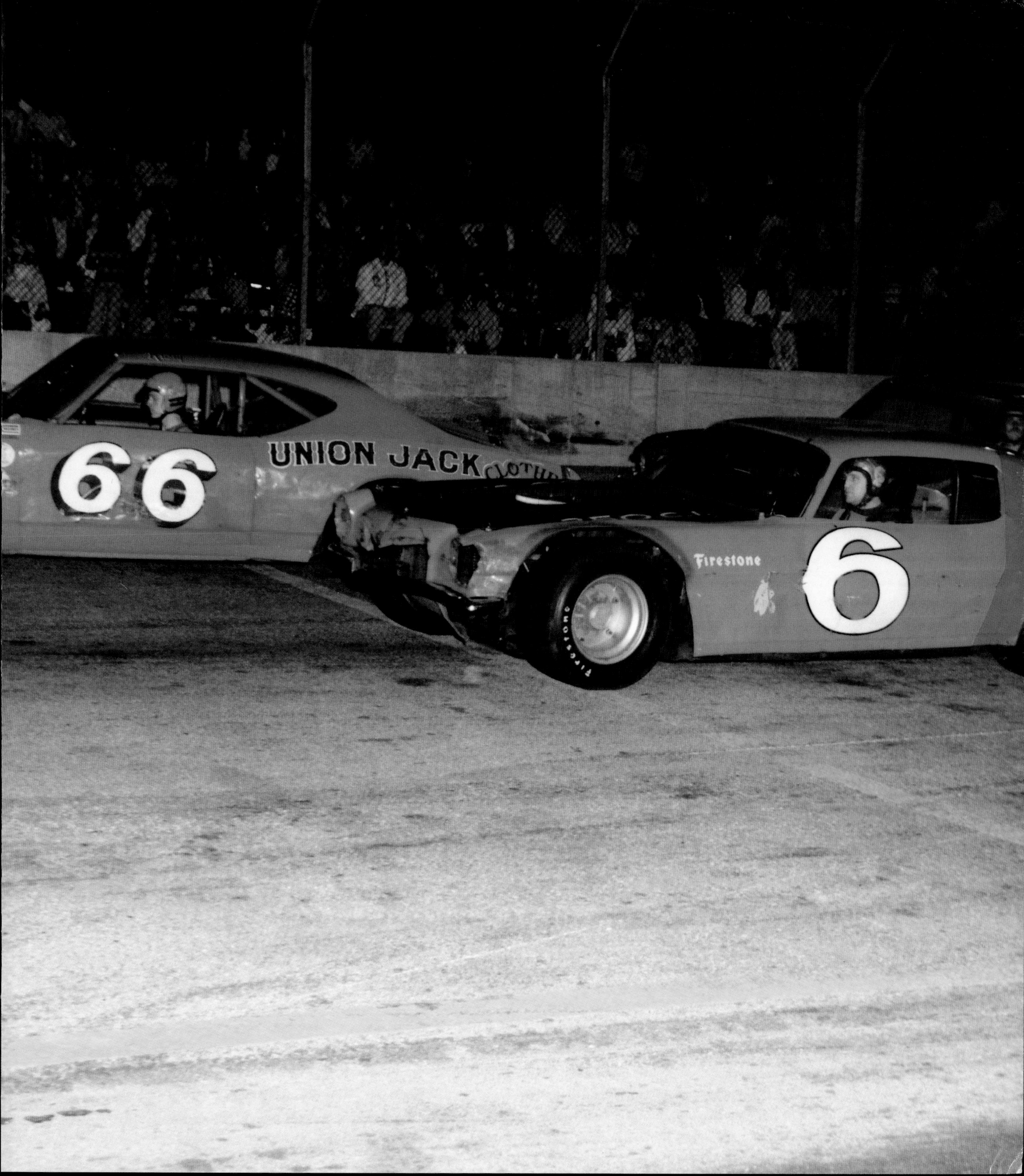
66
UNION JACK
Firestone
6

This is one of eight celebrations Russ and his crew, Mike and Rusty, had in Victory Lane at Tri City Speedway in 1975 after winning weekly feature races. He was track champion that year. Between Russ and the flagman stands Ed Hall, whose daughter, Patti, married Rusty five years later. (Wallace collection)

In 1975, Rusty still raced at Lake Hill, but he did not join his father at Tri City Speedway, a half-mile dirt track on the other side of the Mississippi River in Granite City, Illinois. Russ was just as successful on the Tri City dirt as he was on the Lake Hill asphalt. But Rusty didn't like dirt. He didn't feel like he had control of his car. "Dirt is for plantin' taters," he'd say.

On March 10, 1975, Mike Wallace turned sixteen and, like Rusty, obtained a court order to begin racing. Mike started in the sportsman division and almost immediately began winning. He raced with his father at Lake Hill and Tri City and had no problem adjusting to dirt. Even Judy was behind the wheel in 1975. On May 11, she won a powder-puff race at Lake Hill.

Judy also tirelessly drummed up publicity and support for the family's racing efforts. Almost any help was welcome, considering the family's financial constraints. The Wallaces were never destitute, but they never had much left over at the end of the week. As Mike says, "We grew up with a comfortable lifestyle, not knowing that we didn't have much money."

Judy frequently called Sonderegger to lobby for stories, although in a city as deeply rooted in stick-and-ball sports as St. Louis, the racing news was always relegated to the back page of the sports section. "It was really hard for both Rusty and Ken Schrader to get any notice here because of the baseball and football teams," Sonderegger says. "College sports are big here, too. So they pretty much labored in the shadow of all of that."

The racing at Lake Hill and Tri City was linked through an organization called the Gateway Auto Racing Association. Russ was the association's late-model stock car

The Wallaces were never destitute, but they never had much left over at the end of the week. As Mike says, "We grew up with a comfortable lifestyle, not knowing that we didn't have much money."

champion in 1975 after winning the track championship and eight features at Tri City and finishing sixth in the points at Lake Hill. When the association held its annual banquet at the Machinist Hall in Bridgeton, Missouri, it was a big night for the Wallaces. In addition to Russ's awards, Mike won the sportsman division championship at Lake Hill in his rookie season, as well as the association's combined title. And Rusty finished third in the Lake Hill late-model standings. Rusty won eighteen races on Midwestern short tracks in 1975, including a thirty-lap qualifying race at the National Short Track Championship in Rockford, Illinois. And he won the award there for Best Appearing Car over the 120 other entrants.

But the man to beat at Lake Hill in 1975 was Jerry Sifford. Driving a Boss 302 Ford Mustang, Sifford won eleven features and was nearly unbeatable. Rusty knew Sifford's car well. He had worked on it. Sifford owned a machine shop, and Rusty began working there after he obtained his driver's license.

"I was doing valve jobs and rebuilding motors," Rusty says. "I was running the cylinder head shop. And I was working on race cars." Later he worked for another family friend, Glenn Bopp, a race car chassis builder.

Rusty and his brothers also were gradually taking over the responsibility of maintaining their father's car. "They did a good job," says Russ. "I'd get frustrated with something and throw my hands up and leave. I'd come back, and they'd have it fixed. My brother Gary raced for two years, too, and the boys took care of his car, too."

Russ was never too particular. "My car needs a paint job," he would say. "Could you boys just slap some on?"

Rusty and Mike would reply: "No, we're gonna sand it down and do it right."

Rusty was well tuned to the hottest trends in late-model stock car racing. He was a huge fan of Pete Hamilton, the winner of the 1970 Daytona 500. By 1975, Hamilton was no longer running in the NASCAR Winston Cup series but was still a terror on the short tracks driving a home-built derivative of the Dodge "kit car," a 1970s marketing program that let racers build race cars on Dodge chassis.

"He had this car that he had designed out of a 1968 Camaro front frame section and a Chrysler rear section and a real high-rev motor," Rusty says. "It was incredible to watch him. He was just kicking everybody's butts all the time. So I said, 'I gotta meet this guy.'"

The Wallaces had first seen Hamilton when he raced at Rolla in the early 1970s. In 1975, Rusty drove to Florida to try to visit the master.

"I'm sure he slapped me away a couple of times like someone swatting a fly," Rusty recalls. "But I refused to go away. I was such a nuisance to him. Just a terrible pain. Finally, he *had* to befriend me. So he and his guys finally accepted me and let me hang out with them. And I came back to St. Louis with a burning desire to build a car like Pete Hamilton's car."

But time that might have been spent building race cars instead was expended on repairing vacuum cleaners. Rusty worked at the family business, OK Vacuum, for several years after finishing high school. "I repaired thousands of vacuum cleaners," he says. "You'd have to clean all the garbage out of the bags—chewing gum and lint. It was awful. The biggest problem? They were always breaking belts. I didn't think it would ever stop. It was aggravating because it was completely different than what I was trying to do. I did it way too damn long."

Says Russ: "It was a good income. Rusty didn't want to work there, but it was a job. He did it because he needed the money to race. I've always said that I didn't begin to make any money until I quit racing. And it's true. So we had to work to race. We had two stores. I ran one and my brother ran the other. Rusty worked for my brother. Gary was a lot stricter. But Rusty still wanted to leave all the time. He'd say, 'I've got to work on my car,' or 'I've got to leave for the track.'"

Says Rusty: "It always amazes me when people think I had money to race, because I didn't. When I was a teenager, I used to hunt for Coke bottles with my brothers. We used to cash them in and use the deposit money for racing. We'd spend all day accumulating junk batteries or old radiators and take them to a recycling center to get enough money to buy gas for the truck to get to the races every week."

Russ never ventured far beyond St. Louis to race because he couldn't afford to, and he had a family. Rusty was young and single and did not see why he should have the same constraints. As for money, well, he would find a way to race. And by the end of 1975, he was ready for a change. Lake Hill was a tough little track, but it was a starter speedway. It was a place you had to leave to get anywhere in racing. Rusty knew that. And Don Miller said the same thing.

Miller, a former drag racer, lived in St. Louis. He had stopped racing to raise a family but still came to Lake Hill Speedway from time to time. And in that small fraternity of St. Louis racers, he'd gotten to know the Wallaces. Miller was in the automotive business and knew Roger Penske, who in the 1970s was becoming one of the top car owners in American automobile racing. When Penske offered him a job in 1971, Miller accepted on the condition that he could remain in St. Louis. Penske agreed. Miller was

This blue-and-white Number 66 Camaro is the car Rusty raced at Lake Hill Speedway in 1975. Here he poses inside the third turn with his brother, Mike, and volunteer crewman Mike Lutz. (Wallace collection)

Penske's type—smart, driven, hard-working, passionate about both business and racing, always on the go.

"What I liked about Rusty was the intense fire inside of him. He just wanted to race so badly," says Miller. "It reminded me of when I was in it. It didn't make any difference if I made any money or had to work twenty-four hours a day, I was going to do it. His enthusiasm rekindled my fire for racing. You think he's hyper today? Back then, multiply it by three. He was just wide open. And I liked that. I went to a couple of races to watch him. One thing led to another. Before I knew it, I was trying to help him every way I could.

"He was a good student—a good listener," Miller says. "He knew where he wanted to go. And if he didn't have all the knowledge he needed to get there, he'd seek out someone who did. He doesn't get much credit for being methodical because he's pretty hyper. But he was very methodical. He seemed to bounce from one thing to another, but all the time he was bouncing, he was thinking, too. So I used to sit with him and talk to him about his future."

Miller well knew that Rusty could not blossom as a racer in St. Louis. He would tell neighbors he was involved in racing, and they would reply, "Oh, horse racing?" So Miller told Rusty he had to go where racing people could see him.

"You've got to get out of Valley Park," Miller said. "You've got to get some more experience so that once you get in a more visible series, you don't look bad."

"If everything were perfect, how would I go about it?" Rusty asked.

"First of all," replied Miller, "get on the road and do some racing."

"We almost never paid nobody who worked there because we never had no money to pay them. If they wanted to come with us to the races, as long as they had some food money, we'd take them along."

When Rusty Wallace went on his own to race, his first car owner was a fellow racer named Charlie Chase, who became one of his best friends and remains so today. Chase was such a dedicated car nut, one might have assumed that his business was auto parts or car repair. But when he came out of the U.S. Navy in 1964, he became a St. Louis County fireman. He is a battalion chief today, with thirty-five years of experience.

But Chase was a racer at heart, and he had started at Lake Hill Speedway around 1970, first with modifieds and hobby stocks, then late-models. "Rusty was running into the side of my car all the time," Chase says. "He was just wild—uncontrollable. So I decided I could save a lot of time and money by having him drive my car."

Their relationship actually began in another way. Every Tuesday night in the early 1970s, Rusty, Mike, and Kenny Wallace would load up the family's blue-and-white Chevy Suburban with hundreds of copies of the *Community Press*, a free weekly newspaper, and deliver them in St. Louis suburbs. It was another family job the boys hated.

Long before they turned onto Country Squire Drive and came down his street, Chase could hear the old Suburban headed his way.

"You'd hear the tires squealing, and the muffler would be half off, and they would come down the hill real fast and swing around the cul-de-sac and start throwing papers on the front lawn," Chase says. "A lot of papers. They were tryin' to get rid of 'em anyway, and I'd wind up with fifteen papers."

Chase owned a sportsman car at the time. The Wallace brothers favored their dad's late-model. They would shout a challenge or an insult. Chase, usually working in his garage, responded in kind. Sometimes he'd lie in wait and throw dirt clods at the

Suburban as a dozen newspapers spewed from the vehicle and landed on his lawn. Then the old Suburban would loudly roll back up the hill and disappear.

Outside another house on their route, the Wallaces would see a truck emblazoned with "Penske Racing Products."

Kenny recalls: "Every time we went past that house, we'd look at that Penske truck, and we were just in awe. We would always slow up when we threw the newspaper there." It was Don Miller's home. But the brothers never had the opportunity to meet Miller at his home. Rusty would tell him years later, "I wanted to meet you, but you were never home."

The trips past the homes of Chase and Miller broke the monotony of delivering newspapers. The brothers earned $200 a week for delivering 6,000 newspapers, but it was hard-earned cash. "Every Wednesday, we'd roll 6,000 of them with a 12-volt rolling machine and fill up the whole back of the Suburban," Rusty says. "To this day, the smell of newspaper ink makes me sick. I hate newspapers."

Rusty drove. Mike sat in the passenger seat, throwing papers. "I was in the back," says Kenny. "I was the one who always kept the papers coming up to the front seat so they could throw them. Once we just got tired of it. We wanted to get done early. So we just took them all and threw them in a dumpster. Well, when a few hundred people called and complained, we got caught. Boy, Dad was angry about that one."

Chase soon realized that the old Suburban that came past his house every Wednesday night was the same one he saw in the infield of Lake Hill Speedway every Sunday night.

It wasn't long before Chase got to know the Wallaces. In September 1975, Chase towed his late-model stock car to Rockford Speedway in Illinois for the National Short Track Championships. The Wallaces also went. Before qualifications, Chase went out for a quick lunch. When he returned, he found his car destroyed. His driver, Bob Miner, of Potosi, Missouri (a distinction that led Miller to nickname him "The Potosi Flash"), had stuffed the car into the wall during practice.

"He totaled it," Chase says. "So I came on home and decided to quit racing. But Rusty came over. He said, 'I'll fix the car and we'll go racing together.' I wasn't too keen on that. But I decided it would be cheaper for him to drive it than for him to continue running into it."

Chase, Miller, and the Wallaces all got to know each other at Lake Hill in the early 1970s. It was a mutual friendship, as Miller discovered after the horror of May 5, 1974, at Alabama's Talladega Superspeedway—a day that changed his life forever.

POOR BOY

CHASSIS COMPANY
DES PERES, MISSOURI

A SMALL TOWN CORPORATION... WHERE THEY MANUFACTURE RACE CAR FRAMES, NOT BULLSHIT. "HONEST CHARLIE CHASE", OUR FOUNDER GUARANTEES YOU THE CUSTOMER THAT YOUR HARD EARNED DOLLARS WILL BUY PERFORMANCE NOT TELEPHONE CALLS..... OUR QUALITY IS EXCELLENT.... DELIVERY TIME, SHORT ...AND OUR PAYMENT TERMS SIMPLE.....YES WE EXCEPT

CASH . CASH . CASH . CASH

WE HAVE A DEAL WITH THE BANK THEY DON'T BUILD RACE CARS AND WE DON'T LOAN MONEY......

This is the Wallace family's infamous blue-and-white Chevy Suburban that Rusty, Mike, and Kenny used to deliver newspapers in 1976. This photo is from a Wallace family home movie. (Wallace collection)

"Don was with me doing a Sears Auto Center visit in Birmingham," Roger Penske recalls. "I said, 'Come and help me at the Talladega race. Gary Bettenhausen is going to drive the Matador. I just need you as a gas catch-can man.'"

Bettenhausen ran with the leaders, passing and getting passed for the point. He had led eight times for 35 laps when he pitted on lap 105. Another car had dropped oil on a rain-slicked pit road. Grant Adcox lost control and looped his Chevrolet. Miller was standing behind Bettenhausen's car, manning the gas catch-can, when Adcox slid into him, crushing Miller's lower body between the two cars. Miller was gravely injured. Two other Penske crewmen received minor injuries. Both cars were too badly damaged to continue. Adcox, who died in a crash in the 1989 Atlanta Journal 500, was uninjured, but went into shock.

"Just about every bone in my body from the waist down was broken," Miller says. "I spent seven weeks in an Anniston hospital. They did four or five operations during the first week and finally said they were going to have to take my right leg off." When Miller returned to St. Louis, minus a leg, Rusty and others refused to let him get too down about his plight.

"They knew I used to like to ride motorcycles," Miller says. "And those guys kept bugging me and finally embarrassed me into riding this 250cc enduro bike. So, without a leg and with all these broken bones, I got on that motorcycle, and pretty soon I was riding. To this day, I can't believe it. They helped me recover. What they did was build my confidence."

When the fireman and the vacuum cleaner repairman joined forces in the fall of 1975 to go racing, they had to figure out a way to pay for it. Russ Wallace, for one, didn't think they could do it. He had always raced for fun. That was costly enough. As much as he loved racing, as often as he encouraged his sons, Russ could not imagine how Rusty could make it as a full-time racer.

"How are you going to go racing when you don't have any money?" he would ask

"I'll find a way," Rusty would say. As far as Rusty was concerned, it wasn't even an issue.

With Chase, Rusty saw the opportunity to build the Pete Hamilton–style car he loved so much. He and Chase visited Hamilton again. "Pete helped me design one, and I built it in St. Louis," Rusty says. The chassis and roll cage were finished by November 1975. Around that time, Miller suggested: "Why not build more Pete Hamilton–style cars and sell them?" Rusty was thrilled with the idea. The Poor Boy Chassis Company was born.

Miller arranged to rent half of a building in the suburb of Des Peres, about halfway between Arnold and Creve Coeur. "It was a place for Rusty to maintain his race cars, but it was also the place where we started the chassis-building business," says Miller. Miller kept his street rod there, too, which gave him an excuse to hang out and work on cars.

Says Rusty: "We rented a beat-up building and started building chassis right there where we were working on my race car. There was this guy named Mike Algar—we called him "Alligator"—who ran a speed shop in Springfield, Illinois. He sold parts and pieces to racers all over the Midwest. So he started selling our cars. Guys really liked them on dirt tracks. I built twenty-three of them one year. We sold every one of them."

"Rusty really learned about cars then," Miller says. "I think that's why Rusty is as good a chassis guy as he is. He knows what he wants the car to feel like. He really learned what made them tick because he built them."

The Poor Boy staff was volunteer. The payoff was the opportunity to work on race cars and going to the races with Rusty. This is how Rusty's first team—the Evil Gang—was born.

"Bobby Allison nicknamed us "the Evil Gang," says Miller. "Bobby and I were really good friends. And he became good friends with Rusty, too. Bobby used to call me 'Evel.' He'd say, "You've got more pins in your body than Evel Knievel." Then he started calling the whole group of us the Evil Gang. We were just a crazy bunch of guys who came together. We were always overcoming the insurmountable. That was standard practice."

Says Chase: "We almost never paid nobody who worked there because we never had no money to pay them. If they wanted to come with us to the races, as long as they had some food money, we'd take them along and make sure they had a place to sleep. We'd give them something if we could. But what else could we do? You don't normally go racing on a fireman's salary and the income of a vacuum cleaner repairman.

"The guys would *work*, too. They'd show up every night at six o'clock just like it was a regular job. When I'd get off at the firehouse, I'd go over there and we'd work through

In November 1975, Rusty and "the Evil Gang" finished welding the chassis and roll cage for the first car ever built at Poor Boy Chassis Company. It was a copy of the Pete Hamilton design Rusty was so fond of. Don Miller's cartoon is taped to the front of the car. (Charlie Chase collection)

The first business card for the Poor Boy Chassis Company was created by crew member Dave Wirz. "He went to trade school and knew some gal there learning to be a printer," says Charlie Chase, who saved the one reproduced here. In one year, the company built almost 25 chassis and sold them all, Rusty recalls. (Charlie Chase collection)

Rusty and Charlie Chase are ready to hit the road with a fully loaded truck and trailer in this snapshot taken in early 1976. Working on a shoestring budget, the St. Louis fireman and his driver, a full-time vacuum cleaner repairman, managed to do well enough to win a feature race and the rookie of the year title at Fairgrounds Speedway in Springfield, Illinois. (Charlie Chase collection)

the night until two o'clock in the morning, doing anything we could to make a buck to go racing."

Besides Rusty, Charlie, and Don, the Evil Gang included Mike and Kenny Wallace, both of whom were still in school. "It got to the point where you could see where I'd laid in bed because the sheets were so black," Kenny says. "It was just a nonstop deal. After school, we'd go to the shop, go home, go to bed at one o'clock in the morning, somehow get out of bed the next morning at seven and go to school, go to the shop. . . . I had a sixth-grade teacher pull me aside and—I'll never forget it—she said I smelled like a shop. 'Please take a shower,' she said."

The Evil Gang also included Paul Andrews, Jeff Thousand, and Dave Wirz.

Andrews at age twenty-three became the crew chief and Rusty's first paid employee. Andrews was as steady and reserved as Rusty was hyper. Rusty's first press kit, produced by Don Miller in 1978, quoted Andrews: "Rusty tells the press how many races we've won. I tell them how many we've finished."

Recalls Andrews: "I went to work for Rusty's uncle in the vacuum cleaner store when Rusty worked there. Me and Rusty became friends, and I started working at his shop in the evenings after work. It was a struggle not having the money you really needed. You couldn't just get what you wanted when you wanted it.

"And there were a lot of people telling me I shouldn't be in racing," he says. "It was, 'You're having a good time now and enjoying yourself, but what are you going to do with the rest of your life? You're wasting your career racing.'"

Andrews stuck with it, of course, and was the crew chief for 1992 Winston Cup champion Alan Kulwicki. He was also with Rusty's teammate, Jeremy Mayfield. "That's the biggest thing that sticks out in my mind: 'You can't do that for the rest of your life,'" Andrews says. "Well, yeah, we can. I'm proud of that. No doubt about it."

Thousand had long hair back then, usually tied in a ponytail, and Chase called him "hippie." They met at Glenn Bopp's shop. "He looks the opposite today, but I still call him hippie," Chase says. "But he liked messing with cars. He said, 'I want to go racing. I can weld.' So he became part of the gang and started bumming around with us."

Recalls Kenny: "We used to call him 'blackout' because at midnight he went home and went to bed." Today, twenty-five years later,

As Rusty's new team evolved in 1976 and 1977, the nucleus of the Evil Gang became Rusty, Paul Andrews (left), and Jeff Thousand (right). Andrews was Rusty's first full-time, paid employee. Despite discouragement from family and friends, Andrews stuck with racing and today is a top Winston Cup crew chief. Thousand still works for Rusty today as his head chassis specialist. (Charlie Chase collection)

Before Rusty took his new Pete Hamilton—style Camaro to Winchester for its first race in the spring of 1976, he posed in a park for some publicity photos. At this point, the car carried only three advertising decals—the engine decal for Don Kirn, a decal for D&M Speed Shop, through which the Poor Boy chassis were sold, and a rear-panel decal for Poor Boy Chassis. (Charlie Chase collection)

Thousand, as head chassis specialist, is still a key member of Rusty's team.

Dave Wirz was known as "the Dog." Recalls Miller: "He had this old white Valiant that they used to terrorize lower Arnold with. They called that car the "white dog" because it was real slow. Pretty soon, he became synonymous with it." Wirz came from a racing background. "My father raced stock cars before I was born," Wirz says. "I was helping a guy out at Lake Hill, and I started hanging out with Rusty and his brother Mike. I took care of Rusty's tires. I did a lot of the engine work—adjusting valves and valve springs. But I mainly took care of the tires." Wirz, according to Rusty's first press kit, had a knack for being able to "manufacture those trick parts you just can't buy."

"Ninety percent of it was a volunteer deal," Wirz says. "I lived with my parents and just kinda hung with Rusty. He was very dedicated. He always said, 'Someday, I'm going to be the Winston Cup champion.' He took care of just about everything you needed. He'd buy you gas to get you back and forth to the shop. And he'd give you cigarette money and beer money. If he won a big pile, he'd cut us in on the deal. We all had a pocketful that week to do whatever with. I wasn't making no money. But I didn't need no money."

Wirz also scrounged the first business card for Poor Boy Chassis. "He went to a trade school and knew some gal there learning to be a printer," Rusty says. "So he had her make them up for us."

The Evil Gang also included engine builder Don Kirn, who met Rusty through Chase. The deal was simple: Kirn provided engines and took a third of the prize money.

Rusty was eager to race on the fastest tracks he could find, and for his on-the-road debut, he picked one of the fastest short tracks in existence—legendary, dangerous Winchester Speedway, which was 333 miles east of St. Louis in Indiana. The race was the Memorial 200 on May 31, 1976.

The race started under threatening skies after a heavy morning rain. On lap 10, coming off the fourth turn of the high-banked, half-mile oval, Terry Senneker spun midway through the thirty-car field. Six cars crashed. A fire erupted and spread across the track.

"Ninety percent of it was a volunteer deal," Wirz says. "I lived with my parents and just kinda hung with Rusty. He was very dedicated. He always said, 'Someday, I'm going to be the Winston Cup champion.'"

"We were runnin' pretty good with them—third or fourth—when this crash happened," recalls Chase. "Rusty drove right through it. He came into the pits. I went to him in the car. His eyes were really big."

Both men were shaken, as were Russ and Judy, watching from the grandstand. Chase told Rusty: "If you want to park the car, it's OK. We can load this thing up and go."

"No, no," Rusty said. "I'm all right. We're going to make some money. I'm ready to go."

Rusty reached as high as second before a shock mount broke. He completed 182 of 200 laps, and finished seventh. He remembers the crash well, not for how it affected him, but because "it scared my mom and dad to death."

Another experience in 1976 had a huge impact on him. In February, Rusty went with his family to Daytona for Speedweeks. It was their first visit. They rented rooms on the second floor of a low-budget motel, about as far from the beach as you could get, but it didn't matter. It was Daytona. And this was a racing vacation, as the family's home movies clearly show.

Some of the films show remarkable close-ups, including ones of Cale Yarborough posing with Linda Vaughn and A. J. Foyt chatting with friends. Mike, who showed remarkable resourcefulness, captured these scenes. "Somehow I walked right onto pit road like I owned the place," Mike recalls. "Rusty spotted me. He was hanging on the fence, asking, 'How the hell did you get over there?' I really don't know how I did it, but we had no passes. We knew nobody. I just snuck onto pit road. And I wasn't about to leave. I was playing press guy. The other thing I'll never forget is how much money it cost to get all that film developed."

Recalls Rusty: "My first Daytona 500 was the race where David Pearson and Richard Petty crashed coming off turn four on the last lap. It was wild. We started driving from St. Louis, and twenty hours later we got there. Nobody else drove except for Dad. We'd sit in the grandstands all day long and watch practice. Then we'd go to all of the little hangouts everyone went to and have dinner. And every night, we'd go to New Smyrna and watch the racing there [at Volusia County Speedway] until the wee hours of the morning.

"After the Daytona 500, we stopped at a Burger King, and Pearson's car—the car that just won the race—was sitting there on a trailer, all smashed up. That's how it was back then. You would see stuff like that. It was special. Before I saw that race, I hadn't really paid a lot of attention to NASCAR racing. After that, I knew I wanted to be a Winston Cup driver."

But he was still a long way from that goal.

This is Rusty's infield stall at a track in 1976. When he and Chase began racing, their first race car transporter was Chase's pickup truck, complete with camper shell and everything that could be packed inside. Here Jeff Thousand sits at the back. Kenny stands shading his eyes. "We had three in the front, and I'd lay on the floor under the sleeper just because I wanted to go to the racetrack so bad," says Kenny. (Charlie Chase collection)

The view through the grandstand fence at a speedway in Wisconsin in 1976 shows Rusty Wallace as a cocky, handsome kid with a head full of frizzy hair and an uncommon passion for racing. "Rusty wanted to beat everybody," says Charlie Chase. "And that included his brothers, his father, his friends. He just wanted to beat anybody he could beat." (Charlie Chase collection)

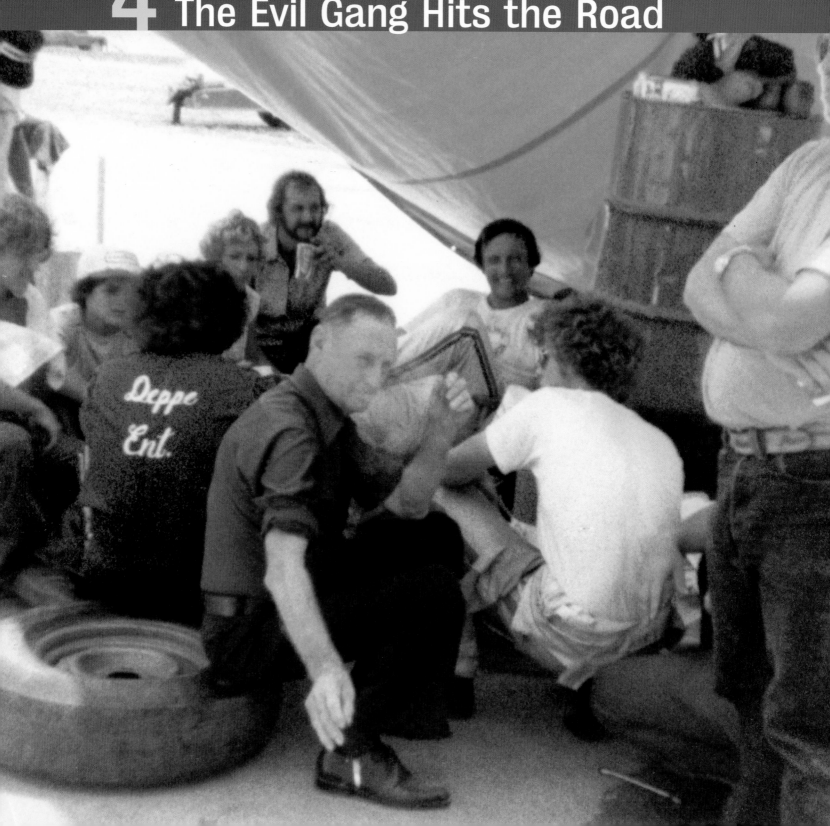

By day, Rusty worked at OK Vacuum. At night he worked on his race car. Sometimes he couldn't tolerate the monotony of repairing vacuums.

Rusty continued to race the Pete Hamilton–style, leaf-spring chassis with a Camaro body through 1977, although he painted it blue for the new season. By this time, the car was regularly being beaten by drivers using chassis made by Ed Howe, a driver and car builder from Beaverton, Michigan. (Charlie Chase collection)

Opposite: There was always time for an infield chat, even in the heat of August. Rusty, with his back to the camera, kneels in this photo as he talks with Larry Phillips under the shade of a sun-blocking tarp at I-70 Speedway in Odessa, Missouri. Rusty turned twenty-one at around the time this photograph was taken in 1977. The following year, he and Phillips raced together through-out the Midwest. (Wallace collection)

One of the legendary short tracks of the 1970s was Fairgrounds Speedway, which was in the Ozark Empire Fairgrounds along Interstate 44 in Springfield, Missouri, 210 miles southwest of St. Louis. Fairgrounds Speedway, along with tracks such as I-70 Speedway, Winchester, Rockford, Five Flags, New Smyrna, and others, attracted not only the top Midwestern and Southern late-model drivers—full-time professionals like Dick Trickle, Dave Watson, Larry Detjens, and Freddy Fryar—but also Winston Cup stars. Bobby Allison came to Springfield, and Donnie did, too. Darrell Waltrip raced at the short tracks from time to time, as did David Pearson.

The Fairgrounds Speedway also had a strong weekly series that was well supported by fans and racers. The racing was on Friday nights, and more often than not it was dominated by Larry Phillips. Springfield was his hometown, and Fairgrounds Speedway was his backyard.

In the spring of 1976, Rusty, Charlie, and the Evil Gang joined the Fairgrounds scene. They would roll up in an old converted bread truck with their blue-and-white Camaro on a trailer. As often as not, they'd be running late, scrambling to get the car unloaded and ready.

"Rusty was the only person I ever knew who could unload his truck before he got to the racetrack," says Phillips, who is still racing—and winning—today. "We always drove like a bunch of nuts anyway, and he'd be whippin' that truck around curves. In the back, all the tools would be coming out of their drawers, and the equipment and stuff would be flyin' around all over the place. When they got to the track, they'd have to spend a bunch of time sorting everything out and putting it back in place."

By June 1976, Rusty was getting in the thick of things at Springfield. He finished fourth in the Friday night feature on June 5. That same weekend, Russ Wallace won his fourth straight feature at Tri City Speedway, where the fans were as hostile as ever.

On June 11, the great Alabama short-track driver, Freddie Fryar, invaded Springfield and stole the feature. But Rusty was fast. Kirby Arnold, the *Springfield News and Leader* motorsports writer, wrote: "The racing Wallace family was at Fairgrounds Speedway Friday to watch Rusty build an early lead, only to spin and finish sixth."

Kenny remembers the night for another reason: "My dad and Mike showed up with black eyes, all beat to hell. They were getting so tired of my dad and my brother winning at Tri City that somebody mouthed off at my dad. It was in a Denny's Restaurant. Of course, Mike jumped up and got in the guy's face. Well, they were some real bruisers, and my dad and Mike got the tar beat out of them. Somebody fired a gun into the air to halt the fight." That didn't stop them from winning. The night after their visit to Springfield, Russ won his fifth straight feature at Tri City, and Mike won the sportsman race.

Stock Car Racing magazine published an article on the Wallaces that month, written by motorsports journalist Al Stilley, that provides a fascinating commentary from Russ. "We race two nights a week and live racing seven days a week," he said. "If [Rusty] had the money, he would be a full-time racer. He wants to race at a lot of places, but right now he doesn't understand dollars. He's a hell of a race car driver, but he also understands a race car. I don't. He knows more about cars now than I did when I was his age. I make up for my lack of knowledge of cars with driving ability. Rusty knows everything about cars."

On June 18, Larry Phillips won the feature at Springfield while Rusty finished fourth. Finishing seventh was a diminutive seventeen-year-old driver from Arkansas named Mark Martin. It may have been the first time they raced together. Martin already knew who Rusty was. When the Evil Gang made its debut at Winchester in May 1976, Martin and his father had admired Rusty's new, bright-red Camaro from the grandstands. "His stuff looked so good, I thought he was a rich kid or something," Martin says. "He had a beautiful car, and all his guys had matching red pants and shirts."

Martin's most vivid memory of Rusty in Springfield was that "he spun out a lot at first. Plus, he didn't fasten his deck lid down, and whenever he spun out, the deck lid would blow up. And it would really look ridiculous."

Bicentennial weekend—the celebration of the United States' 200th birthday—was a

wet but memorable occasion at Fairgrounds Speedway. The Firecracker 101 was scheduled for Friday, July 2, but rain postponed it to the night of the anniversary itself, Sunday, July 4. A brief power failure had darkened the facility earlier in the evening. Now, as the twenty-one-car field lined up for the feature, it happened again. A transformer outside turns three and four suddenly blew. The lights there went out, replaced by a spectacular waterfall of sparks from the overworked transformer. The unexpected fireworks show put a crimp in the racing until someone had a bright idea.

"A driver suggested fans direct the headlights of their passenger cars onto the darkened turns," reported the *Springfield News and Leader*. "They practiced a little bit, but shortly after midnight voted not to race."

Rusty's first feature win at Springfield came on Friday night, August 24, 1976, in a thirty-lap event sponsored by the local radio station, KTTS. He beat the field by half a lap. He poses in victory lane with the trophy girl (left) and Teri Kezar, a nineteen-year-old woman motorcycle jumper who safely jumped over a string of cars but was 8 feet short of the record. (Charlie Chase collection)

After a second postponement, Larry Phillips won the Firecracker 101 on Monday afternoon, July 5. Rusty finished seventh.

Rusty was fast that summer but also prone to trouble. He was listed only once—a third in a heat race—in the race results published in the *News and Leader*.

"You don't see anything about us because we did horrible," Kenny says. "We were wrecking every week or blowing up, or something was happening." But the disappointments were soon forgotten in the daily grind. By day, Rusty worked at OK Vacuum. At night he worked on his race car. Sometimes he couldn't tolerate the monotony of repairing vacuums.

Recalls Chase: "Rusty would always sneak out the back and come by and get me, and we'd go to the shop or spend the afternoon at the motor shop talking with Don Kirn, our engine builder. He'd get yelled at, but it didn't stop him."

"Every Friday, we would take off work at 3 p.m. and we'd all meet at the shop as quickly as we could," says Kenny.

"I used to wait for Patti to get off work at Dohacks Restaurant so she could go along," says Chase. "She was the greatest. She had to put up with six guys. Six guys and Patti."

As the summer of 1976 wore on, Rusty's luck improved. He finished third in a Saturday night feature at I-70 Speedway in Odessa, Missouri, on August 7. And on August 28, two weeks after his twentieth birthday, he broke into victory lane at the Fairgrounds. The evening's schedule included a nineteen-year-old woman motorcycle jumper named Teri Kezar, but Rusty stole the show.

"Rusty Wallace, although only twenty years old, drove to an easy victory Friday night at Fairgrounds Speedway," the *News and Leader* reported. He took the lead on the sixth lap and had stretched it to a half lap when the checkered flag fell on lap 30. The victory helped Rusty become 1976 Rookie of the Year at Fairgrounds Speedway.

The 1977 season started like 1976 ended. On April 3, Phillips swept his heat race, the trophy dash, and the feature in Springfield. Rusty finished second but led the first ten laps. In June, Rusty finished fifth in one of the three 100-lap American Speed Association (ASA) races at I-70 Speedway. In July, he finished third in the Missouri State Championship at Springfield and battled with Mark Martin before Martin won the Arkansas state championship at Tri-State Speedway in Fort Smith, Arkansas.

In September, Rusty competed in the World Cup 400 at I-70 in a race that included

the legendary black NASCAR driver Wendell Scott, but he did not finish. A tire problem at the Rockford Speedway in late September sent him reeling to seventeenth place in the National Short Track Championship. He raced in the Robbins 500 at Nashville, Tennessee, in October. He raced near Chicago. He raced in Wisconsin.

"I was all over the country," Rusty says. "I had my team. And we had the Hilton. We lived in the Hilton. We were broke all the time. But we were having a great time. By God, we saw the country."

On June 26, 1977, Rusty competed in the Triple Crown 300 ASA event at I-70 Speedway in Odessa, Missouri. He finished fifth in the first 100-lap segment, eighth in the second 100, and fourteenth in the third 100. His Poor Boy chassis, as it turned out, was dynamite on dirt but not as quick on asphalt as a new design by racer Ed Howe. (Wallace collection)

The year 1977 also marked the debut of Rusty's new transporter, a red panel truck dubbed "the Hilton" because of the homemade sleeper compartment in the front of the vehicle. This snapshot shows the Hilton and Rusty's Camaro in 1977, pulling into a Mars self-serve gasoline station outside St. Louis in another of the seemingly endless journeys on the road. (Wallace collection)

The Hilton was an old bread truck that served as their race transporter, their shop on wheels, and, as the name indicated, their hotel. The team had installed a wall about halfway back. The front portion was the living quarters; tools and parts were in the back.

"We put a bed in there—a couch—and two captain's chairs, and, of course, a stereo," says Chase. "We had a TV in there, too, and I used to sit on the motor cover, watching TV and talking."

Everyone shared the driving duties. "I would play Norvel Felts music when I was driving if I got tired," Chase recalls. "His voice would just drive you nuts, so I would play his songs over and over again to stay awake while driving down the road, drinking coffee. They hated it. They played what I called 'narcotics' music—stuff like Poco and Traffic."

Even Kenny, who was fourteen in 1977, took his turn. "Kenny could drive, so we let him," Chase says. "I know his dad didn't like it, but sometimes we would drive through the night to get to the next race, so everybody who could drive drove. We'd be sprawled all over the place, sleeping, and Kenny would be driving full bore. We could get the Hilton to go 80 or 90 miles per hour, and sometimes he'd drive it full bore right through a radar trap.

"So he'd suddenly say, 'They're comin!' and one of us would take his place. He'd stand up and someone else would grab the wheel and sit down and take the ticket. Most of the time we tried to get Dave Wirz to do it, because he was the littlest and looked more like Kenny. This happened five or six times."

Since they were almost always low on money, the Evil Gang opted for low-budget motels when they did stop.

"At the Super Eight in Springfield, the top floor was $8 a night. The middle was $9 a night and the bottom was $12 a night," Chase says. "If we did good, we stayed down on the bottom. If we did bad, we stayed up top." One room generally slept four.

"I can't tell you how many motels they beat out of the bill," says Russ. "They had to sometimes or they couldn't survive. I helped him all I could. But I didn't have that kind of money. I loaned him money for a motor one time. I tell you what—the money

At the gas pumps outside his Valley Park shop, Rusty stands with Dave Wirz behind his car. Rusty occupied half the building in the background. The other half—and the gas pumps—were owned by Jimmy Calicutti, who operated a crankshaft company. In December 1982, this entire area went under 8 feet of water when the Meramec River flooded. (Wallace collection)

Outside Rusty's new shop on St. Louis Avenue in Valley Park, Rusty, Jeff Thousand, and Dave Wirz (left to right) prepare Rusty's Camaro for another trip to Springfield in 1977. Barely visible in the background on the right is the Wallaces' infamous two-tone Chevrolet Suburban that bombed through Creve Coeur every week as the Wallace boys delivered the *Community Press.* (Wallace collection)

"Sometimes when I'd get to a motel and give 'em my credit card, they'd take the thing," Rusty recalls. "I'd say, 'Hey, give me my card back.' And they'd say, 'The bank says handcuff that thing.' "

situation—I just didn't know how the hell he was going to do it. We were blue-collar people. It bothered me to be too close to it. Nobody made any money racing back then. There was no money to be made. Many people went into bankruptcy over racing. It took their family earnings."

Judy often came to Rusty's rescue. "I used to pay his phone bills," she says. "And I've give him my credit card on the weekends in case anything happened. I just couldn't send my kids off out across the country without a credit card."

Judy was a film inspector at Swank Motion Pictures in St. Louis. "They rented 35-millimeter films to nursing homes and colleges and places like that," she says. "When the films came back, I'd have to check and make sure there weren't any cuts or breaks or heavy scratches."

"She kinda kept her own money," says Russ.

"But I wound up spending more money on them than I realized," Judy says. As for the credit card, "Rusty never abused it. He just kept it full," she says.

That might not have been the case with all his cards.

"Sometimes when I'd get to a motel and give 'em my credit card, they'd take the thing," Rusty recalls. "I'd say, 'Hey, give me my card back.' And they'd say, 'The bank says handcuff that thing.' So I'd have to use another one. But we were broke all the time. I'll never forget, I went to Jackson, Mississippi, for a big 200-lapper, and I had a spare carburetor. And this guy named Billy McGuinness wanted it so bad, I sold the carburetor to him for three hundred bucks. And I said to the guys, 'Man, we got enough money to get home.' Then I went out and won the damn race. Won nearly $10,000, I think. We went to a bar that night, and I think we spent every nickel of it."

By the end of 1977, Rusty knew he had to make some changes. It had been a flat year as far as results. Team records show that Rusty entered thirty-five major events and had twenty-one top-ten finishes but won only three races. The Pete Hamilton chassis design was outstanding for dirt tracks. "But I found that every time I took my Pete Hamilton car asphalt racing, I was getting beat," Rusty says. "And all these cars that were outrunning me were Howe cars. Ed Howe was a driver and car builder from Michigan, and he used to blow me away. But Larry Phillips was building a copy of the Howe car at his shop in Springfield. Larry had a company called Performance Parts Company, and he was a Howe distributor. I started hanging around with Larry. He knew my dad and liked my dad a lot. And he liked me a lot. So he said, 'You know what, kid? I'm going to take you under my wing. But you gotta do exactly what I do and exactly as I say. We'll build you a car just like mine, and we'll go on the road and race 'em at the same races.' So Larry and I built me a car just like his and we took off.

"When I went with Larry, that ended the Charlie Chase era. I bought him out for $6,000. I think I had a thirty-year payment plan. It seemed like $40 million back then. But basically, I had a payment plan. And I paid him. I bought him out and went on racing."

Says Chase: "I was running out of money. I couldn't continue. They were getting on

me at work. I was coming in tired. Rusty and I were very close friends at that point, and I had to make a decision. I had to decide whether I was going to be a fireman or a professional racer."

The team was trying to race on only $10,000 a year, and it just wasn't working. Not when crashes and repairs had to be factored in. Circumstances helped push Chase over the edge.

"I can remember that it happened in Springfield," Chase says. "The week before, Rusty had demolished the car—totally wiped it out. He had been following Phillips. They were going through the pack. The door closed on him and Phillips both, and they both got wiped out. So we came back to St. Louis and worked all week—the whole week—and built a whole new car. We were working right up to the time we left for the track.

"We called down there, and they said to come on. They said they'd hold the feature up a little bit. So we put it all together. And we worked on that thing on the way down there. We got there just in time, and we're following Freddie Fryar going into turn three, and Freddie blew a motor. Rusty hit the oil and then he hit the wall. He knocked the front end off of it and the back end, too. We had that car together for a total of about three hours, and here it was, wrecked again.

"Rusty got out of the car and laid in the grass. We all thought he was hurt. So we went running down there as fast as we could. And when we got there, he wasn't hurt. He was just layin' in the grass, almost crying, because the car was demolished again. Right after that, I decided to get out."

"He started with nothin', and he raced with nothin'. But he had enthusiasm. His eyes just glittered. He had the 'want to.' Before the year was up, he was hard to beat."

This 1971 photo from a Wallace home movie shows Larry Phillips in Springfield, Missouri getting ready to load his No. 74 race car onto a trailer. Phillips and Jerry Sifford were transporting their cars to Florida for a race. Russ was also scheduled to make the trip, but a recent crash had broken his left leg. (Wallace collection)

Opposite: At twenty-one, Rusty was living his dream: He was racing for a living. This 1978 snapshot caught him in the pits at Nashville Speedway with a section of tailpipe in his hand. Although most of his racing was in Missouri and Arkansas, he ventured elsewhere to race when his schedule allowed it. (Charlie Chase collection)

No driver has made his mark in American short-track stock car racing quite like Larry Phillips. With only one Winston Cup start to his credit, Phillips is unknown to most followers of big-time NASCAR racing. But for more than thirty years, Phillips has been racing and winning at small and smaller ovals all over the Midwest, West, and South. His record of five championships in the NASCAR Winston Racing series is unprecedented.

Phillips always drove basic race cars. "It would be all stock parts," recalls Chase. "He used to go home and leave his cars over at the garage that Kenny Schrader's dad owned in front of Lake Hill Speedway, so everybody would go over there and start looking at Larry's car. And they would see all stock stuff. There was nothing special."

Phillips's legacy is particularly remarkable because he tutored two of NASCAR's greatest stars—Rusty Wallace and Mark Martin.

Wallace was first, and Phillips was fond of the exuberant young driver from St. Louis who wore his hair in a big, bushy, frizzy, Afro-like mop that looked like, in Don Miller's words, "an explosion in a bear factory."

"I've always had a place in my heart for Rusty," Phillips says. "He started with nothin', and he raced with nothin'. But he had enthusiasm. His eyes just glittered. He had the 'want to.' But he had no money. All of us were so poor we could barely buy the tubing to build these cars. I knew he didn't have any money. But I knew his dad and mom, Russ and Judy. And you could just see his enthusiasm boiling over. So at our shop in Springfield, we built him a frame and cage and gave it to him. He paid for all of the accessories and came to our shop and assembled the car. And he went racing with me for a year. We would race at the Fairgrounds Speedway on Friday night and Fort Smith, Arkansas, every Saturday. Before the year was up, he was hard to beat."

As Russ sees it, this is when Rusty really learned to race.

"At first I never thought he was going to make it as a driver," Russ says. "He was not aggressive enough. But after that one summer he went with Larry Phillips, he was a completely different racer. He was almost too aggressive then. But that's where he learned. He started winning then."

"He didn't have to be taught anything," Phillips says. "I didn't know anything to teach him. We raced as hard as we could. I think it was the equipment. He had what it took."

Whatever the reason, the change was obvious almost as soon as the season started. On March 31, Rusty and Larry finished first and second in Springfield in the year's second weekly feature race. "The trophy dash gave the fans quite a thrill as they watched Phillips tailgate Wallace through the entire race, but Wallace held his ground and took the victory by half a car length," reported *National Speed Sport News*.

The next night, at Tri-State Speedway in Fort Smith, Phillips again won the main events, capturing a pair of 30-lap features, but Wallace made a last lap charge in the second race and won the trophy dash in another close duel. "The overflow crowd was on its feet," the paper reported.

To learn from Phillips, one simply followed him.

"Larry Phillips would always have to start at the back of the pack, but it would only take two or three laps and he would be in front," recalls Chase. "Phillips was a mastermind in traffic. The big deal was to follow Phillips through traffic. He knew where the holes were. A couple of times the holes closed and we crashed. But after a while, Rusty started getting really good at it. And that's when he started winning."

This 1978 portrait of Rusty in his racing uniform became the file photograph of Rusty at *National Speed Sport News* and was reproduced dozens of times that year and over the next few years. (Wallace collection)

In the feature at Springfield on April 7, Rusty led the first lap. Phillips started in the back but passed everyone except Rusty on the first lap. On the second lap, he passed Rusty, who finished third. The next night, in Fort Smith, Rusty led for a time but spun and finished fifth. Phillips won his third straight. But Rusty was getting close. The whole team could feel it. They had worked hard to reach this new level. Their anticipation was keen as they fled their jobs at 3 p.m. Friday, April 14, piled into the Hilton, and headed toward Springfield.

Wallace was the odd man out of the spotlight as the evening got under way. Phillips and Mark Martin were pitted against each other in a five-lap match race for $500. Martin had barged into Springfield the previous year and started beating Phillips on a semiregular basis. The fans went berserk; finally, a new winner. But in the match race, Phillips beat Martin.

This is yet another version of the Pete Hamilton leaf-spring-chassis car Rusty raced on the ASA circuit just before Larry Phillips gave him a Howe-style chassis. No detail was overlooked, from the gold-painted wheels to the carefully riveted headlight covers. This snapshot shows the car sitting in the garage in Valley Park. (Charlie Chase collection)

WALLACE RACING ENTERPRISES

923 ST. LOUIS AVENUE
VALLEY PARK, MISSOURI 63188

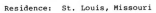

RUSTY WALLACE - DRIVER

Residence: St. Louis, Missouri

Birth Date: August 14, 1956

Marital Status: Single

Height: 5 feet 11 inches

Weight: 170 lbs.

Russel (Rusty) Wallace, 21, is currently one of the most promising young racing drivers in short track stock car racing.

Rusty, a native of St. Louis, Missouri, is the eldest son of Russ Wallace, Sr., (5) five time Tri-City Speedway Late Model Stock Car Points Champion.

Rusty, who is a veteran of several hundred short track stock car and modified racing events, started his racing career at age sixteen (16). Wallace recalls, "My first racing experience came on motorcycles, stock cars came later." Rusty competed in the (AMA) American Motorcycle Association - Moto-Cross series from 1970 to 1972, where he won (4) four out of (7) seven Regional Championship events.

Wallace made the switch to stock car racing in early 1972, when with financial aid from his family, he purchased a 1969 Chevelle Short Track Racer. Rusty competed in the (CARA) Central Racing Association Short Track Championship at Lakehill Speedway, St. Louis, Missouri, where he was voted most popular new driver. Wallace was also awarded the CARA Most Improved Rookie award.

Wallace continued to compete in CARA events during 1973 and at the wheel of his 1969 Chevelle earned the coveted Central Auto Racing Association "Rookie of the Year" award.

He then went on to build a 1972 Camaro for the 1974 CARA Short Track Championship Division. The 1974 CARA Short Track Late Model Racing season saw Wallace lead the points championship for most of the season, eventually finishing (2) second in points at seasons end.

This is the first page of a two-page press release about Rusty that Don Miller prepared at the beginning of the 1978 racing season. Miller was always diligent about sending every release to the racing papers and spent considerable time developing a rapport with *National Speed Sport News* publisher Chris Economaki. (Don Miller collection)

The back panel of the car was reserved, as always, for an advertisement for the Poor Boy Chassis Company, which remained in business after Chase sold out. Poor Boy was now making race car trailers as well as chassis. (Charlie Chase collection)

It's a Friday night in 1978 at Fairgrounds Speedway in Springfield, and the racing is about to get under way. This was Rusty's championship season at Springfield. He also won the track title at Tri-State Speedway in Fort Smith, Arkansas. (Charlie Chase collection)

In practice, Rusty was quick, too. And just before the feature, Rusty had bought four new Goodyear tires. At that time, everyone was running Firestone tires. When the green flag fell, Rusty took the lead. And then he ran away from Martin, Phillips, and everyone else. Martin was a distant second, Phillips was third.

As he took the checkered flag, Rusty was ecstatic, waving out of the window with his left hand. Kenny and Paul Andrews jumped off the tool box and began running toward victory lane.

"It was a hell of a race," Rusty recalls. "And after I won the thing, I was so excited about it, comin' down the front straight, I've got my hand out the window and I'm waving to the fans and hollering and—*boom*—right into the damn wall! It was, 'Hello, Rusty.' "

As the *Springfield News and Leader* reported it: "The St. Louisan took the checkered flag as he approached a group of slower cars. With no place to go, the Chevrolet Camaro spun and backed into the first turn wall. Wallace, though, promptly threw it into gear and drove—the wrong direction—back into the pits, the car's left front dragging on the asphalt and the twisted rear aiming high in the air."

"It was a big wreck, too," Rusty says. "I tore the front end up, and we had to work all night long putting the rear frame section back on the thing and getting ready for Fort Smith the next night. It was humiliating as hell—me walking around feeling like an idiot. But that's the one we always joke about."

The team was successful in its all-night vigil, because Rusty was almost as strong at Tri-State as he was at the Fairgrounds. After a seesaw battle with Phillips, Rusty pulled even with him in the final turn. They thundered to the checkered flag side by side. Phillips won by a fender.

Five days later, on page fourteen of *National Speed Sport News*, Rusty Wallace was headlined in two stories. Rusty's name had been printed in *Speed Sport* many times, but usually in connection with his father. This was the first time Rusty was featured for his own accomplishments in the national paper of record for motorsports.

Wallace shows up Fairgrounds hot shots

By KIRBY ARNOLD
Staff Writer

Remember all the pre-race hubbub about the big clash between youngster Mark Martin and veteran Larry Phillips in Friday night's late model stock car program at the Fairgrounds Speedway?

Toss it.

Phillips was beaten by a youngster all right but not by the 19-year-old Martin.

Instead, 20-year-old Rusty Wallace broke through the traffic early and held on for victory in the 25-lap feature.

Phillips opened the evening with a car-length victory over track champion Martin in their much-publicized five-lap match race, but ran second to Martin in their heat race and placed third behind Martin and Wallace in the trophy dash.

Phillips and Martin did have their moments in the early laps of the feature before Martin pulled in front and placed second by a comfortable margin.

Wallace, who Phillips contends is the fastest-rising young star around, never received a challenge...that is, until after he already had crossed the finish line. The St. Louisan took the checkered flag as he approached a group of slower cars. With no place to go, the Chevrolet Camaro spun and backed into the first turn wall. Wallace, though, promptly threw it into gear and drove — the wrong direction back to the pits, the car's left front dragging on the asphalt and the twisted rear aiming high in the air.

Phillips and Martin commanded the attention at the start, even though Wallace was tracking down Willard's Jay McIntosh for the lead.

Phillips, who started behind Martin, gave the Batesville, Ark., driver a tap in the rear as they took the green flag then opened a wide margin the first lap.

Then, Phillips dropped back to Martin's side to set up a bumper-to-bumper duel between the two for second place. Martin, who greeted Phillips' bumper with his own a few times, made his move around the outside and took second place on the 15th lap.

Jim Campbell, Harrison, Ark., also had a tough battle with Marionville's Wayne Woody and placed fourth by a narrow margin. Behind Woody were Marionville's Fred Tiede and McIntosh.

It was the first feature Phillips has lost in four weeks of racing at the Speedway this season.

Another new face hit victory lane in the mini-stock feature — Springfield's Rolland Arnold. Arnold also got off to a quick start and finished well ahead of Roger Arnhart, Kansas City, Kan.

Arnhart, who also hadn't lost a feature, was caught in traffic early.

LATE MODELS
First heat — 1. Bob Johnson; 2. Charlie Kinnard; 3. Jay McIntosh. Second heat — 1. Mark Martin; 2. Larry Phillips; 3. Rusty Wallace. Consolation — 1. Wayne Woody; 2. Fred Tiede; 3. Jim Campbell. Trophy dash — Martin. Feature — 1. Wallace; 2. Martin; 3. Phillips; 4. Campbell; 5. Woody; 6. Tiede; 7. McIntosh; 8. Darrell Holt; 9. Kinnard; 10. Bill Allen; 11. Ray Felker; 12. Roy Hanson; 13. Johnson; 14. Kenny Smith; 15. Roy Taylor; 16. John Ward; 17. Cornelius.

MINI-STOCKS
First heat — Rolland Arnold; 2. Rick Pope; 3. Roy Nelson. Second heat — 1. Roger Arnhart; 2. Paul Campanelli; 3. Jerry McCall. Consolation — 1. Ron Love; 2. Forrest Tindle; 3. Tom Bray. Trophy Dash — Love. Feature — 1. Arnold; 2. Arnhart; 3. McCall; 4. Love; 5. Pope; 6. Campanelli; 7. Scott; 8. Nelson; 9. Bray; 10. Tindle.

Above: This is the story of Rusty's famous win-and-crash victory at Springfield as reported by the *Springfield News and Leader* on April 15, 1976. (Don Miller collection)

In 1978, the Evil Gang became a powerful force in late-model stock car racing and a threat to win everywhere they went through the Midwest and South. As the group poses in front of a freshly painted Hilton, engine builder Don Kirn sits next to Rusty while standing, from left to right, are Kenny, Jeff Thousand, Dave Wirz, and Mike and Paul Andrews. (Wallace collection)

Ironically, another future great driver also earned his first prominent play in *National Speed Sport News* that week. His article was on page fifteen, facing Rusty's stories. The headline said: "Dale Earnhardt Nets First Cumberland Feature." Two days after Rusty's breakthrough, Earnhardt had won a 100-lap late-model feature at Cumberland County Speedway in Fayetteville, North Carolina.

On April 29, 1978, Rusty won for the first time in Fort Smith. With lightning flashing across the sky that Saturday night, Rusty set the pace in qualifying, which meant he started in the back. He sliced through the back markers and was fifth by the second lap. He took over fourth on the fourth lap, third on the fifth lap, and the lead on lap 7. The victory gave him the points lead at Fort Smith. That same weekend, Earnhardt won his second straight seventy-five-lapper in Fayetteville.

Rusty and Phillips continued to battle with each other and Martin through May. On May 12, Martin crashed while trying to again pass Phillips for the lead at the Fairgrounds. Rusty was second. One week later, Rusty dusted the entire field, nearly lapping even Phillips, who finished second.

"The thing I always remember about Springfield is passing Mark Martin in the grass," Rusty says. "Going into turn one, I would just go right down in the grass and pass him. He would get so mad. And the next time he would do it to me."

Phillips has fond memories of his travels with Rusty. "Kenny is the real hero," he says, laughing. "Rusty liked to have worked Kenny to death. It was slave labor. But he stuck with it."

"My job was to change gears and do the brakes," says Kenny. "We had drum brakes then, and I had to pull all of them off, clean them up, and reassemble them."

"You have to understand Kenny," says Chase. "He was always running around asking, 'What are you doing here? How does that work?'" And he was always saying, 'Let me do it; I want to do that. I can do it.' He could be a pain in the ass. And you could tell when Rusty would get tired of baby-sitting Kenny."

Wallace Chases Phillips Hard For Fort Smith Feature $

FORT SMITH, Ark. — Veteran Larry Phillips has found his dominance of the late model class at Tri-State Speedway threatened by Rusty Wallace.

Phillips, Tri-State's most winning driver, was able to hold off Wallace by less than a fender to win his fourth straight feature of the 1978 season Saturday.

Wallace Well Oiled at SFS

By BEVERLY EDWARDS

SPRINGFIELD, Mo. — Rusty Wallace topped well known Larry Phillips and Mark Martin to capture his first late model feature at Fairgrounds Speedway Friday evening.

Wallace took the lead early in the 25-lap event and maintained it by a good margin, never to be headed by young Martin or Phillips. After taking the checker, Wallace hit the second turn wall.

Martin and Phillips battled over second spot with Martin finally pulling away from Phillips. Jim Campbell and Wayne Woody challenged each other for fourth with Campbell winning by a light margin.

The evening's events were started with a five-lap $500 match race between Martin and Phillips. Phillips took the checkered flag with Martin right on his bumper. Martin took the dash and fast car heat. The second heat was won by Bob Johnson.

The mini stock division saw a new face in victor lane also. Local ace Roland Arnold captured the feature with point leader Roger Arnhardt taking second. Ron Love took the dash and heats went to Arnold and Arnhardt.

This is the first loss of the season for both Phillips and Arnhardt with their three-race winning streaks ended.

Larry Schild finished third with Glen Hurt fourth, Chuck Knight fifth, Dr. J.D. Busby sixth, Dickie Walton seventh and Bill Dillard eighth.

Wallace led the first five laps of the 25-lap feature before Phillips could grab the lead. Phillips then paced the field until lap 22 when Wallace again moved into first place.

Wallace's lead lasted for only one lap before Phillips got back into first. However, the race was not over as Wallace made one last bid to take the checkered flag first. On the last lap, Wallace pulled even with Phillips going through turn four.

With the two sprinting for the flag stand, Phillips was able to edge out Wallace by less than a fender as the two Camaros flashed by the flag stand.

Tilly Evans took his second straight street stock feature while Johnny Johnson captured his first sportsman feature of the season.

Wallace, Johnson and Vernon Reese were trophy dash winners.

The April 19, 1978, edition of *National Speed Sport News* carried the news of Rusty's first feature win for 1978 at Springfield, a race in which he crashed after taking the checkered flag. (Don Miller collection)

"I don't want to be Rusty Wallace from Tri-State Speedway in Fort Smith, Arkansas," Rusty said. "I want to be like A. J. Foyt. I need to get out there and run with some of the big boys."

"Well, this one time, I had a motor home, and we were all eating at a restaurant in Fort Smith. Kenny went to the bathroom and told Don Kirn to tell us. But somehow the signals got crossed, and we left while Kenny was in the bathroom. We thought Kenny went with his brother Mike. And they thought he was with us."

"I couldn't get the toilet paper off the roll," Kenny says. "And when I finally came out, everyone was gone. So I decided to walk home. Only problem was, I went down the wrong ramp. I was headed toward Florida."

"Then he thought about it," Chase says, "and called his mom and dad in St. Louis and said they left him. We had to send a guy back down from Springfield to find Kenny, pick him up, and bring him on up to us."

This sort of mishap didn't bother Russ and Judy as much as the dangers of the highway. "We worried about them going down through the mountains to Fort Smith more than racing," Judy says. "That was a pretty wild trip." U.S. 71 from Fayetteville, Arkansas, to Fort Smith was considered one of the most dangerous stretches of highway in the United States.

"A lot of people have been killed there, and it's a wonder we weren't killed there, too," says Phillips. "Sometimes the most exciting part of the trip was going over the mountains back and forth from Fort Smith to Springfield. We drove like a bunch of nuts. But we never had any wrecks."

On May 27, disaster struck, not on the highway, but on the track. It happened on the seventh lap of a fifty-lap feature at Fort Smith. "Larry and I were at the back of the pack because they always started the two fastest guys in back," Rusty says. "Larry got ahead of me, maybe two cars ahead of me, and something happened and somebody spun."

Phillips had just pulled below Terry Deatheridge in the third and fourth turns to pass for the lead when he ran into the car that had spun. Deatheridge plowed into Phillips, and the cars burst into flames. The carburetor snapped off Phillips' car, but the electric fuel pump kept pumping fuel. Five drivers, including Phillips, were seriously burned.

"Rusty drove right through the fire," says Kenny. "But it was so intense, it singed Rusty's face a little bit and the nose of his car, which was made out of plastic, was melted a little bit."

In November 1978, Russ posed with his three sons. Rusty and Mike are wearing Penske Racing jackets provided by Don Miller. By this time, Russ had curtailed most of his racing. Mike was still racing at Lake Hill but was beginning to venture out as Rusty had. (Wallace collection)

"Larry got trapped and couldn't get out of his car," Rusty says. "And when he finally jumped out of his car, his uniform was on fire. We were there before any help. So we're patting down his uniform and getting the fire out. His goggles were melted to his face. Larry was like Dick Trickle, always drinking coffee and always smoking a cigarette. Larry would have a cigarette in his mouth while he was racing, and a cigarette lighter in the car."

"Larry didn't have no gloves on at that time," says Kenny. "And what I'll never forget is seeing the skin literally falling off Larry Phillips's hands. And he was saying, 'Give me a cigarette.' He still wanted to smoke. And we piled him into a little Chevy Chevette and ran him to the hospital because there was only one ambulance, and another guy was hurt even worse." It took years for the burns to fully heal, but Phillips was racing again by mid-August.

The race was stopped for forty-five minutes. The promoters considered calling it off. But the drivers voted to race. The event was shortened to twenty laps. Rusty won easily. And in the weeks that Phillips was recuperating, Rusty went on a rampage. On June 9, he won at Springfield, beating Martin. The next night he won his third feature of the season at Fort Smith. And on Sunday night, he won back home at Lake Hill Speedway— his second feature victory there.

He headed to Fort Wayne, Indiana, for a Wednesday night race at Baer Field Speedway and won that event as well, passing Bobby Allison for the lead on the sixth lap. And then he won again at Springfield and at Fort Smith on June 16 and 17. In nine days, he had won twice in Springfield, twice in Fort Smith, once at Lake Hill, and the 100-lapper at Fort Wayne.

Then he started winning in other series. On July 2, Rusty ran away from Dick Trickle and the field in a seventy-five-lap ARTGO race before a record crowd at Capital Super Speedway, a half-mile track in Oregon, Wisconsin. *National Speed Sport News* described Rusty as "one of the hottest late-model drivers in the country right now." And he must have had the big crowd on edge, because he arrived late, no doubt with the engine already warm. (If the Evil Gang knew they were going to be late, they'd duck into a rest stop and throw Kenny into the driver's seat of the race car while it sat on the trailer so he could warm up the engine before they reached the track.)

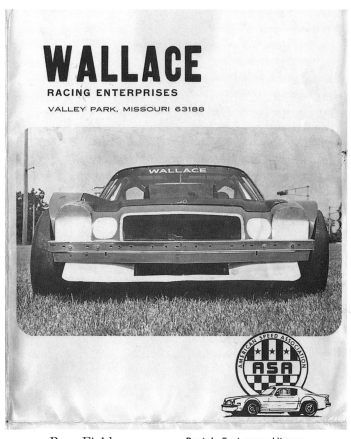

Rusty's first press kit was assembled by Don Miller around 1978 and was way ahead of its time, at least for a racer at Rusty's level. Miller wrote season reviews and previews and issued them on custom-made letterhead. He always made sure to mail the news releases to *National Speed Sport News* editor Chris Economaki, who sometimes mentioned the rising star in his weekly column. (Don Miller collection)

Third Main To Wallace

SPRINGFIELD, Mo. — Rusty Wallace chalked up his third late model feature win of the season Friday night at the Fairgrounds Speedway.

Mark Martin looked to be a threat after taking his heat and the dash but could not catch Wallace and had to settle for second. Only third place Bob Johnson was on the same lap with the flying young duo.

Vester Cales and Russ Phillips rounded out the top five. Cales captured the other heat.

Wallace Is LM Winner

VALLEY PARK, Mo. — Rusty Wallace chocked up his second late model feature win at the Lake Hill Speedway Sunday night. Paul Lawson was second and Len Gittemeier placed third.

Wallace was also the top qualifier for the evening's races with a 15.86 clocking. Heat winners were Lawson, Mike Wallace and Rick Bayer. Wallace won the handicap race and Fred Stotler won the B feature.

Rick Harding won the street stock feature

The excitement spread that summer to wherever Rusty and the Evil Gang towed his car. On July 11, a Tuesday night, a huge crowd filled Rockford Speedway to watch Rusty battle Trickle before finishing second. Visiting Neil Bonnett finished third. The next night Rusty was back in Fort Wayne, Indiana, for an ASA race at Baer Field. Lap after lap, Rusty battled side by side with Butch Miller for the lead. But on lap 74, Miller's car broke a right front hub. Miller crashed head-on into the outside wall of the third turn. Rusty went on to win. It was his first ASA victory.

In late July, Rusty won the Race of Champions 400 in Birmingham, Alabama, beating Darrell Waltrip, among others. All the while, he continued to win at Fort Smith and Springfield. On August 26, he won his heat race, the trophy dash, and his fifth feature victory of the season to clinch the 1978 late-model championship at Tri-State Speedway. In September, he clinched the late-model title at Fairgrounds Speedway.

The 1978 season had been Rusty's best. He entered ninety-three events and won twenty-three features and ten poles. He had forty top-five finishes and a 90 percent finishing rate. As the new year loomed, he huddled again with Don Miller to talk about his career.

"I don't want to be Rusty Wallace from Tri-State Speedway in Fort Smith, Arkansas," Rusty said. "I want to be like A. J. Foyt. I need to get out there and run with some of the big boys."

"If you want to be like Foyt, why not go race with him?" Miller said.

Miller and Rusty considered the ASA series, which is where Martin went. But they opted for the USAC stocks. "The USAC stock car series was fading, but it had Foyt," Miller says. "And it took him to bigger markets."

There was another advantage. The series raced at some big, fast tracks, like Ontario Motor Speedway in southern California, a copycat of the 2.5-mile oval at Indianapolis, and Texas World Speedway, a 2-mile banked track. Rusty decided he would race USAC in 1979 while cherry-picking other races throughout the Midwest and South.

"You need to plan your career, Rusty," Miller told him. "You don't want to move too fast, but if we do this right, one day your name will be a household word."

"Rusty had never driven one of the USAC cars on the dirt, so he went to A. J. and asked him what the setup should be. This is how much nerve he had."

Rusty made his USAC debut in March, 1979 at Ontario Motor Speedway in Southern California driving his new Pontiac Firebird. He qualified eleventh at 149.452 MPH on the 2.5-mile oval and finished fourth. Mark Martin also competed, but he spun in oil and crashed. (Charlie Chase collection)

Opposite: "I drove well at Talladega and at Charlotte, so I see no reason why I will not do well at Texas," Rusty told reporters before the start of the USAC season finale race at Texas World Speedway in October 1979. With a look of determination and a Pepsi, he strides through his pit stall. (Charlie Chase collection)

To meet the challenges of the USAC stock car series in 1979, Rusty decided to build a new car.

"I went out to California and met with a guy named Tom Hamilton," Rusty says. "Tom was building a chassis that was almost identical to Pete Hamilton's. But instead of using a stock Camaro front frame, his was custom-manufactured and looked more like the race car frame we use now. Everything was identical to the Pete Hamilton car except the front section was handmade. So I bought one and put everything on it the way Pete had taught me."

And instead of using a Camaro body, Rusty attached the body of a Pontiac Firebird, which was 8 inches narrower in the front and aerodynamically superior. Rusty's number 66 Pontiac Firebird became one of the most successful and versatile cars he ever built. It performed well at nearly every track he took it to. It was fast from the dirt at DuQuoin to the high banks of Talladega.

Rusty's debut came in the second race of the season on March 25 at Ontario Motor Speedway in Southern California. Foyt had won the first race in his backyard at Texas World Speedway. Rusty had missed it because he was still building his car.

The California race was Rusty's first on a large, high-speed raceway. But his new car was quick, and he had no trouble adjusting. He had come prepared with plenty of advice from Bobby Allison. Rusty qualified eleventh in the twenty-one-car field. He finished fourth. Foyt won again. It was Rusty's first race with the legendary driver—the winner of Daytona, Indianapolis, and Le Mans. But Rusty wasn't intimidated. He relished the opportunity.

Today Rusty and Foyt are good friends. Rusty helped Foyt field a car for the inaugural Brickyard 400 at Indianapolis Motor Speedway in 1994. Foyt has invited Rusty to hunt at his Texas ranch. But in 1979, the brash young rookie raised the ire of the veteran a time or two, especially when Foyt lost.

Even in that first race, Foyt taught Rusty some lessons. At one point, Rusty was drafting Foyt, who was leading, so he could make a pit stop when Foyt did. But when Rusty wasn't expecting it, Foyt cut a hard left turn and dove onto pit road. By the time Rusty recovered, he was blocked by other cars on pit road. He dropped back to ninth. He eventually fought his way back to fourth, won $2,500 and "did a little better than break even" on the California trip.

Between USAC races, Rusty raced in other series. He competed in ARTGO events in Wisconsin and Minnesota. He made a last-lap pass to win a feature race at Springfield. And on May 4, he made his debut at the biggest, most fearsome speedway of all—Talladega. The race was the Talladega 300 Grand American race, the companion event to the Winston 500 Winston Cup race.

Don Miller, who had lost so much at Talladega, joined Rusty in Alabama.

"Just tell me about this place," Rusty said to Miller. "I don't know what to expect."

"I've been on this racetrack with Mark Donohue at close to 200 miles per hour," Miller said. "And Rusty, I'm going to tell you right now, running down there into turn one is like running down into a big, black tunnel. But it's a big corner. And all of a sudden, you flip sideways and go around the corner. What you gotta do is sneak up on it."

Miller recalls today: "I could tell Rusty was really apprehensive. He was saying, 'Oh, man, this is going to be something. This is going to be something. OK, I'm going to sneak up on it.' So he went out and made one lap and came back in. And I could see that his leg was jumping up and down inside the car. I told him to take it easy. But he insisted he was going to be OK. And on his third lap, he was running close to 200 miles per hour. But that first lap was kind of like shock therapy. It was like taking somebody and throwing him in a cold pool of water and then dropping a radio in there with him."

Rusty qualified third for his first Talladega race. He slipped back to tenth after the start but charged back and took the lead on lap 10. He led five laps. And in

After he made a successful first start at Talladega in May 1979, Rusty moved on to Charlotte Motor Speedway on October 6 in the World Service Life 300 race for NASCAR late-model sportsman cars. Here his Pontiac Ventura, which Bobby Allison owned, sits on pit road before the race. (David Chobat)

Rusty did well at Charlotte. Here he races to the inside of Junior Crouch and Bill Dennis. He finished sixth in a forty-four-car field in his first race at the 1.5-mile oval. (Don Miller collection)

"A. J. wouldn't say a word to me after the race. The week before, when he won and I finished seventeenth, he treated me like a little brother or something."

the final circuits, he battled with eventual race winner John Anderson, smacking fenders. Both cars got sideways. Both drivers made great saves. When the checkered flag fell, Rusty was fourth behind Anderson, Dave Marcis, and Bobby Allison.

After Talladega, Rusty was primed and ready on June 23 when the USAC stockers visited Illiana Speedway, a paved short track in Schererville, Indiana, for a pair of seventy-five-lap races. Rusty was the fastest qualifier. And he won the first race. His first USAC victory came in almost routine fashion. He took the lead on lap 40 and cruised from there. He was headed toward another easy victory in the second race, leading the first 55 laps, when the oil pump failed and his Firebird came to a stop on the track.

On August 11, at Wisconsin State Fair Park in Milwaukee, Rusty had another close encounter with Foyt. Rusty was battling with Joe Ruttman for the lead when they tangled and spun in turn one, giving Dave Watson the victory. Rusty crossed the finish line in second. But Foyt protested, claiming Rusty improperly passed him after spinning. The protest was allowed. Rusty was dropped to eighth.

Rusty was not looking for a fight. He approached Foyt. "He was a little hostile at first, but then he started talking about this race and that race, and pretty soon he wasn't even upset," Wallace told a reporter a few months later. "We had quite a long talk."

Foyt was having one of his finest seasons not only in stock cars, but in Indy cars as well. By mid-August, he had won five Championship (Indy) car races as he marched to his seventh season championship. Then in August, he won back-to-back stock car races in Springfield, Illinois, and Milwaukee.

Foyt seemed a good bet for a third straight win as the series arrived at the DuQuoin State Fairgrounds in Illinois for a 100-lap race on August 25. DuQuoin was special to Foyt. He won his first major victory, which he referred to as his big breakthrough in racing, there in 1960.

There was no reason to think Rusty would be a threat at DuQuoin. It was a dirt track. Rusty had run only one dirt race. It had been at Tri-City with his father several years earlier, and it

Rusty had some of his greatest successes in the late 1970s and early 1980s at the flat 1-mile oval at the Wisconsin State Fair Park outside Milwaukee in West Allis. This photo shows him at Milwaukee in 1979, when he won a USAC race on September 9. "Man, that car just worked so good on those flat tracks," Rusty says. "It had a lot of grip. And we practiced there a lot, too." (Wallace collection)

was enough to convince him he hated dirt. Rusty almost didn't go to Illinois. But he was fifth in USAC championship points, and skipping this race would cripple any chance for the title.

"Rusty had never driven one of the USAC cars on the dirt," Miller says. "So he went to A. J. and asked him what the setup should be. This is how much nerve he had. Well, A. J. gave him the setup, and Rusty gets out there and proceeds to whip A. J.'s ass and everybody else's, too. And afterwards, A. J. was saying, 'Who is this snot-nosed kid?' From then on, it became a real battle."

"It was a dry, slick track," Russ recalls. "If it had been wet, Rusty would have lost. But it was almost like asphalt." Rusty led the final forty-three laps and won by a second over veteran Don White. Foyt finished fourth.

"The track was dried out," Rusty recalls today. "So I drove around the bottom. A. J. and Don White and all the veterans, they're running around the top of the track on the

Although A. J. Foyt protested, USAC spiced its stock car points championship by adding an extra race in October at Rusty's home track in Springfield. Rusty won the first seventy-five-lap race in the KTTS 150. Here he celebrates with the trophy girl and his crew. From left are Kenny, Dave Wirz, Mike Mitler, Bill Childs, Paul Childs, Don Kirn, Steve Scheer, and car owner John Childs. (Don Miller collection)

cushion. So I drove on the bottom, passed 'em all, and drove on. And after the race, they're like, 'What the. . .?' "

"A. J. wouldn't say a word to me after the race," Rusty said in an interview in 1979. "He just hopped into his rent-a-car, slammed the door, and burned rubber leaving the pits. The week before, when he won and I finished seventeenth, he treated me like a little brother or something."

On September 9, Rusty won his second straight USAC race when the series returned to Milwaukee. He beat NASCAR veteran Ramo Stott on the 1-mile flat oval by 3.1 seconds, as nearly every other points contender, including Foyt, had mechanical trouble. A half-hour after the race, some of Foyt's crew, none too pleased with the outcome, stopped by Rusty's pit area.

"Just wait till Texas," they said. "We're going to blow your doors off."

"I'm not trying to make anybody mad," Wallace replied. "You guys are the old pros. I'm just a rookie. I'm just trying to get a start. I don't want any trouble."

In this photo of the last lap at DuQuoin State Fairgrounds, Rusty lets his Firebird slide ever so gently as he held off tough USAC veteran Don White in the Number 93 Dodge Aspen. Rusty had been bold enough to ask the legendary A. J. Foyt for the correct suspension setup at the track, then went on to beat him soundly, leading the final 43 laps of the 100-lap event to win. (Don Miller collection)

The victory at Milwaukee vaulted Rusty from fifth to second in the championship, although he was still a distant 450 points behind Foyt. But Foyt skipped the next race, which was at Illiana Speedway. He didn't have the proper car for a paved short track. Besides, he had a cushion in the points race. And even after Ruttman won and Rusty finished fourth at Illiana, Foyt still had a commanding 300-point lead over Rusty. To win the title, all he had to do was start the final race at Texas World Speedway.

But USAC decided to throw another hurdle in Foyt's path. In late September, USAC stock car supervisor Billie Saxon added a race to the schedule—a pair of seventy-five-lappers at Rusty's home track in Springfield on October 14.

Foyt cried foul. "I think it was pretty unfair," he told *National Speed Sport News*. "If they want a different stock car champion, I'll give [the title] to them." He skipped the race. Rusty won the first seventy-five-lap segment. Joe Ruttman won the second race and overall event. Foyt's points lead over Rusty dropped to 150 points. Ruttman was 190 behind. Now both had a fighting chance.

In the days before the Texas race, reporters asked Rusty about racing against Foyt for the title. Recalls Miller: "Rusty actually got more press that weekend than A. J. did."

"Now A. J., he's never run against a car like the Firebird before, and I've beaten A. J. in this car twice," Rusty told reporter Brad Buchholz of the *Waco Tribune-Herald*. "So I know I can beat him again."

"A. J. and all of his cronies wanted to kill me," Rusty recalls. "They thought I was this big-mouthed kid. Well, the reporters wanted an answer, and that was the answer. Besides, I thought I *could* beat him. So we qualify, and A. J. is on the pole with a new track record, and I'm in second. And we start side by side."

Foyt took the lead at the green flag, with Rusty close behind. Bobby Allison also moved into contention. Soon a battle at the front was raging between Allison, Foyt, Wallace,

KTTS AM-FM 150

USAC National Championship Stock Car Race

Rusty Wallace

The leading candidate for 1979 USAC Stock Car 'Rookie of the Year' honors, Rusty is challenging A.J. Foyt for the National Championship. He won both the DuQuoin, Ill. 100-miler and the Governor's Cup 250 at Milwaukee, Wis. in his Childs Tire Firebird.   —photo by Major Baynes

Springfield Fairgrounds Speedway   *Springfield, Missouri*

October 14, 1979

Official Souvenir Program   50¢

This is the cover from the four-page program for the extra race that USAC added to the 1979 stock car season. It gave Rusty another opportunity to close the gap between him and A. J. Foyt in the championship points battle. Wallace won the first of two seventy-five-lap segments but was seventh in the second segment and finished fourth overall. (Don Miller collection)

Richard Childress, and others. One lap before halfway, Rusty's engine exploded. It was all over. Eight laps later, Ruttman's engine blew, ending his threat. Foyt cruised the rest of the way, finished fourth, and won the championship. Allison won the race.

"It was very disappointing," Rusty says. "I was second, and I had a chance to win my first championship in my rookie year. And then I blew up. I slipped from second to third in the championship, just behind Bay Darnell. It was tough. But I did win rookie of the year."

In December, Rusty headed south for one last race before Christmas. He finished second in the Snowball Derby at Five Flags Speedway in Pensacola, Florida. Meanwhile, Don Miller traveled to Reading, Pennsylvania, for Roger Penske's annual Christmas party.

Miller lobbied Penske to put Rusty in a stock car and enter the NASCAR Winston Cup race at Atlanta—the fifth race of the upcoming season. He knew Penske had a brand-new Banjo Matthews chassis sitting in his race shop in Reading gathering dust. "Lend us the chassis," Miller said, "and we'll put the engine in it and build the car."

Penske had fielded cars in the Winston Cup series in the 1970s. Bobby Allison won three races in 1975, including the Southern 500, driving Roger's AMC Matador. But after the 1977 season, Roger dropped out of NASCAR to concentrate on his Indy car program.

"We talked about it," Miller recalls. "And after a couple of glasses of wine, he said he thought that might be something to do."

But Penske told Miller that if he was going to do it, he wanted to do it right. "Go test at Atlanta first," he said. Penske also wanted to meet Rusty. So on January 29, 1980, Miller and Rusty visited Penske. Rusty was nervous. Penske put him at ease immediately.

"I've been checking you out," Roger told Rusty. "I think you're capable of driving our cars."

For once, Rusty hardly said a word. Penske did almost all of the talking. Rusty said later that Penske was so full of energy, it seemed as if he talked without breathing.

The team included Miller, Don Kirn, Kenny, of course, and Tex Powell, a veteran NASCAR mechanic, who was the crew chief. Jay Signore, the general manager of Roger's racing efforts, also helped out. The team painted the Chevrolet Caprice body blue and white and affixed the number sixteen. Penske's Chevy dealership in Detroit was the sponsor.

Opposite: Not long after this pit stop, Rusty's chase of A. J. Foyt for the USAC title came to an end. His engine blew after 62 of the 125 laps. Foyt, who had won the pole, cruised to a fourth-place finish and the stock car championship. (Charlie Chase collection)

Here Kenny Wallace, flanked by two other members of Rusty's crew, hovers over the engine compartment of Rusty's Firebird as they prepare for the run for the USAC championship in the final race at Texas World Speedway. (Charlie Chase collection)

"Don't let go of it," Allison said. "Keep in full control through that turn, or it might get away from you. The car is not as stable as you think."

Penske owned part of the International Race of Champions series, and when Rusty tested at Atlanta in February 1980, the IROC cars were there as well. Atlanta was one of the fastest, most fearsome tracks in the Winston Cup series. But Rusty relished high-speed tracks. And he gained extra experience at Atlanta when Signore let him test-drive IROC cars.

During the test, Rusty was quite comfortable in his car. Although the Caprice body was not considered as slick as the Monte Carlo or Oldsmobile bodies, this car was fast. The test went surprisingly well. On February 25, three weeks before the race, Miller sent Penske a two-page memo. He said the Caprice, as expected, was slower than the Monte Carlos and the Oldsmobiles, but it was consistent and predictable. With a bit more bodywork on the car, Miller thought Rusty could qualify in the top ten. He concluded: "I believe we could run in the front pack all day and, with a little luck, finish in the top five." His prediction was bold beyond belief, but Miller was not feeding Penske a line. Rusty was fast. And Miller saw no reason why he wouldn't run well on race day.

It was Rusty's first 500-mile race, and he worked hard to mentally prepare himself. Usually, he was hell-bent on getting to the front. For this race, he knew he had to drive the car hard, but very carefully. Rusty was fast, just as he had been in testing, and he won the seventh starting spot. To his right was Richard Petty. Buddy Baker was on the pole in his Harry Ranier Oldsmobile at 166.212 MPH.

But engine problems plagued Rusty's car. As Kenny explains: "Don Kirn, our engine guy, built a good motor, but it kept leaking oil at Atlanta. And you can't run a 500-mile race leaking oil." The engine overheated during the final practice and, as *National Speed Sport News* publisher Chris Economaki reported, "The [new] engine in the unsponsored Wallace Caprice was assembled in bits and pieces." Powell took parts from the qualifying engine as well as an engine rented from Foyt. He had other pieces flown in.

Race day was March 16, 1980. With the extra effort from Powell and the crew, the car was ready. Penske flew in. "You don't have to prove anything to me today, Rusty," he said. "I wouldn't have hired you if I didn't think you were a good race car driver."

That put the rookie at ease. Donnie Allison helped, too. Before the race, he told Rusty to watch out for turn four. The car would feel so good in the apex of the turn, Rusty might relax too much, he said. "Don't let go of it," Allison said. "Keep in full control through that turn, or it might get away from you. The car is not as stable as you think."

Rusty soon learned that Allison was right. The car felt perfect in the heart of the turn. But the exit was a bit sharp, and he could feel the car try to break loose. All afternoon long, he held the wheel tight through that turn and silently thanked Donnie Allison for the tip.

Rusty's only significant problem came in the pits. He ran into the back of Benny Parsons coming down pit road shortly before halfway. Parsons had slowed suddenly. Rusty slammed on his brakes but hit him anyway. Parsons' car crashed into the pit wall

Wallace to renew chase of Foyt

BY BURT DARDEN
Chronicle Staff

At the Fair Stock 150 in Milwaukee Rusty Wallace and Dave Watson were running at a blistering pace when the 23-year-old Wallace spun out.

The top candidate for the United States Auto Club rookie of the year did a 360-degree turn and burst back on the track. He never did catch Watson but the native of Arnold, Mo., figured equaling his best finish ever — a second-place — wasn't that bad after spinning out.

However, A.J. Foyt filed a protest, claiming Wallace pulled in front of him after he spun out. The protest was allowed, Wallace penalized a lap and took home eighth-place money and points.

"A.J. wouldn't say a word to me after the race," recalls Wallace. "He just hopped in his rent-a-car, slammed the door and burned rubber leaving the pitts. The week before at Springfield (Ill.) when he won and I finished 17th he treated me like a little brother, or something."

The next race — the Governor's Cup Race, a 250-miler at Milwaukee — Wallace drove into the winner's circle a second time. Foyt finished 14th.

"Some of Foyt's pit crew came up to me about a half hour after the race," says Wallace. "They told me, 'Just wait until you come to Texas. We're gonna blow your doors off!'"

"I told them I wasn't trying to make anybody mad," says Wallace. "I told them they were the old pros and I [was] trying to get a start. I'm just a rookie. I don't [want to be un]able."

[His confron]tation with Foyt's crew surprised Wallace. [It was] when Foyt had filed the protest at Milwau[kee he] had talked with Foyt in the pits.

"[He was a] little hostile at first but then he started [talking about] this race and that race and pretty soon I [was really] upset," recalls Wallace. "We had quite a [talk]."

[He adm]its he respects Foyt's driving ability but [that re]specting the way Foyt acts at times is [hard].

"[Foyt is k]ind of a superstar and I look up to him," [says Wallace.] " I'd like to be like him. I don't want to [be his pers]onality but I'd like to be able to drive like [him and make] the kind of money he does.

"[When it c]omes to the day when I can't sit down and [relax, then,] well, I think I'll hang it up."

[Wallace h]as been driving professionally since he was [16. His dad] was a race car driver and from ages 13-15 [he work]ed in the pits for him.

"[Dad bought a] second race car and he gave it to me [for my 16th b]irthday," says Wallace. "I had some of my [school b]uddies working for me in the pits. I'll never [forget my fir]st race. I won a 30-lapper at Lakehill Speed[way in St. Lo]uis. I've been going wide open after every[body since th]en."

Wallace hoping to spoil A.J.'s trip to the banks

By JOHN BARKER
Staff Writer of The News

COLLEGE STATION, Texas — The Texan 250, along with two Texas Races of Champions, will close the schedule for the year Sunday at Texas World Speedway.

The Texan 250, a 125-mile event on the high-banked, 2-mile track, may be the best of the season.

Although A.J. Foyt, the defending champion in the USAC stock car division, holds the lead in points, three other drivers, Rusty Wallace, Joe Ruttman and Bay Darnell, could beat out the Houston rancher.

Foyt has 1,640 points, Wallace 1,490, Ruttman 1,450 and Darnell 1,370. Wallace is given the best chance of unseating the defending champion.

THE YOUNGSTER, who turned 23 Aug. 14, is in his first year of USAC stock competition and twice has beaten Foyt. He defeated A.J. in a race at Milwaukee and again in an event at Du Quoin, Ill.

The 5-11, 175-pound driver has won four races, unheard of for a rookie on the high-banked speedways. Wallace also has three NASCAR races under his belt — one at Talladega and two at Charlotte.

"I drove well at Talladega and at Charlotte, so I see no reason why I will not do well at Texas," said Wallace. "If everything goes the way I think it will, I don't see how I can finish worse than second.

"I think I can beat Foyt. He's one of the best . . . the best in the world. I can't bluff him, but I will say we are ready.

"I've talked to some fine drivers who have raced [h]ere against Foyt and they tell me to be ready because [Foy]t will be ready.

"I CAME DOWN here to beat him, even though he has been nice to me and helped me a lot."

Saturday afternoon, Foyt won the pole position with a speed of 170.293 mph. Thirty minutes later, Wallace won the outside front-row starting position with a speed of 170.253, only one-hundredth of a second slower than A.J.

Since Wallace lives on the outskirts of St. Louis, he was asked if he followed either Cardinal team (football or baseball).

"Man, I'm so tied up in what I'm doing, I don't know anything about football or baseball," he answered.

"I got my license to race the day I turned 16 and I'm just now getting to where I want to be. Believe me, winning the championship means much to me and that's what I'm after."

THERE WILL be four NASCAR drivers in the field who may have a say in who wins what — veterans Bobby Allison, Richard Childress, Terry Labonte and Elmo Langley. Several Texans, in addition to Foyt, will be in the 250, including Jimmy Fingers, Tom Williams, Eddie Scott and Ricci Ware Jr.

Fingers is the defending champion in the Race of Champions. There will be two TROC events.

Sunday's schedule calls for the first TROC race to get the green flag at 1 p.m. The Texan 250 will go off at 2 p.m. and the second TROC event will follow.

Tickets are available at the Texas World Speedway ticket office.

Rusty stole the prerace headlines—and irked A. J. Foyt—when he predicted he could beat Foyt in his own backyard and win the USAC title. (Don Miller collection)

Rusty was ready to go in practice for the Atlanta 500 on a chilly March morning in 1980 at Atlanta International Raceway. For safety, Rusty, who was twenty-three when this photograph was taken, sits in a custom-molded seat that provided far greater protection against whiplash injuries. (David Chobat)

and was too badly damaged to continue. Rusty escaped with minor grille damage. He apologized to Parsons after the race. The veteran wasn't happy but understood it was an accident.

Rusty never led a lap in his first Winston Cup race. But he was never out of the top ten either. Although he lost time in the pits, he kept moving up as others had trouble. And when leader Cale Yarborough fell back with distributor problems, Rusty found himself in second, trailing only Dale Earnhardt. He couldn't believe it. Here he was, just trying to get along the best he could, and he was almost leading. It felt so good to be running up front with the biggest names in stock car racing—Allison, Yarborough, Petty. He could imagine them looking at this strange car and thinking, "Where did this kid come from?"

And after 3 hours and 42 minutes of racing, Rusty drove under the checkered flag 9.55 seconds behind Earnhardt. His second-place finish wasn't a victory, but it was bigger than any victory he'd had thus far.

"I was amazed at how good he was—his understanding of the car and the way he drove it," Penske says. "We just missed winning that race by a little bit. And when you bring a rookie to Atlanta, which is not the easiest place to run at, and you're getting him to drive a different car, well, it was a great weekend."

It was a big weekend for Earnhardt, too. His team's morale had been low. This was his first superspeedway victory and only the second victory of his career. After this win, his career took off. The Atlanta 500 was the first of five victories for Earnhardt that year on his way to his first Winston Cup championship.

Rusty thought his career was taking off, too. Penske had said he would run five races with Rusty in 1980. "Maybe now we'll have to reevaluate that," Rusty said after the race. "This is where you want to be. I know I'm going to like this league."

In one of the finest debuts in the history of the Winston Cup series, Rusty finished second to Dale Earnhardt in the 1980 Atlanta 500, which was held on March 16. Here Rusty's grille shows the effects of the collision he had with Benny Parsons on pit road. The crash put Parsons out of the race but did not seriously affect Rusty's car. (Don Miller collection)

"So I slapped him upside the head to wake him up. And when he woke up and saw that he was on fire, it scared him so bad, he threw up on himself and put the fire out."

Rusty had a knack for driving fast no matter what the car or series. This was the car he raced in the ARTGO series, which mostly ran in Wisconsin and Minnesota. The series was designed to be simple and low-cost, as was evidenced by the standard bodywork. The series did not allow the exotic, swooping front snouts that were making their way into the ASA series. (Wallace collection)

Opposite: When the green flag fell in the Alabama 300, Rusty and Richie Evans shot out ahead, trading the lead back and forth. Rusty led 60 of the 113 laps. Evans led 51 laps. Neil Bonnett, the only other leader, was in front for 2 laps. Then rain halted the race for 45 minutes. (Wallace collection)

After his spectacular Winston Cup debut at Atlanta, Rusty dove right back into a frenetic schedule, racing in four different series. He resumed racing USAC. He did some All-Pro races. He also competed in selected ASA and ARTGO races, as well as a few Friday night features in Springfield.

"It was a remarkable thing," Miller says. "I tell people today, and they don't even believe it. But if you had three cars parked here and they were all different, he would figure out a way to run all three of them. And it would be in the same week, too. He did that a lot."

In February 1980, several weeks before his first Winston Cup race, Rusty ran his Pontiac in the Sportsman 300 at Daytona, but finished thirty-third when his engine blew on lap 35. Just one week before the Atlanta event, he raced in the Texas 250 USAC race at Texas World Speedway, finishing third after leading twenty-nine laps. He finished third in a USAC race at Trenton, New Jersey, in mid-April, then won again at Illiana Motor Speedway.

Rusty was racing full time, and his main sponsor in 1980 was John Childs, a racing enthusiast who owned Childs Tire Company in O'Fallon, Missouri. He had met Rusty at Lake Hill Speedway. "I just basically helped sponsor him with tires and money," Childs says. "It seemed like I paid a lot of bills back then. I liked to race. I was hoping to make it pay for itself, but it wasn't too profitable. We couldn't get enough sponsorships."

On May 3, Rusty took his USAC car back to Talladega for another Alabama 300 Grand American race.

"That turned out to be one of the best races I've ever seen," Miller says. "It came down to a battle with the great modified driver, Richie Evans, on the last lap. At the end, Rusty was turning laps at 202 miles per hour in that car. And that was the same car he won with on the dirt at DuQuoin."

The Alabama 300 resumed after the rain and the stage was set for a thirteen-lap showdown. Rusty and Evans ripped off laps exceeding 200 MPH as they came toward the finish. Rusty blocked Evans in the third turn of the final lap and won by two car lengths. (Don Miller collection)

Rusty proudly poses in victory lane after one of his biggest victories—and unquestionably his fastest. Rusty averaged 169.659 MPH in a race that was slowed by only two yellow flags. He earned $11,800 for the win. (David Chobat)

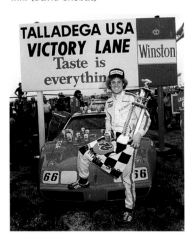

Rusty won by two car lengths after fighting off Evans's attempt to pass in the third turn. "I know they say it's best to be second going into the final lap because of the draft, but there was no way I was going to let him pass," Rusty told interviewers in victory lane. "It's too much work to get out there and lead, only to lose the race on the last lap. I talked to a lot of crew chiefs, and they all say the best thing to do is stay low and make the other guy go outside. And that's what I was going to do."

But nothing was more important to Rusty in 1980 than his races in Penske's Chevy Caprice. His second chance to drive it came in mid-July at a Twin 200 event for ARCA stock cars and CART Indy Cars at Michigan International Speedway. Rusty qualified second and led twice for seven laps. But on lap 81, as he was leaving the pits, his driveshaft broke.

"A couple of the crew guys were upset with me because leaving the pit area, I revved the motor," Rusty says. "They thought I revved the motor so much it broke the driveshaft." Although it was later determined that the driveshaft broke because of a part failure, Rusty's effort with Penske was beginning to sour. Powell was no longer with the team, and the chemistry wasn't right anymore.

Rusty didn't even get to race the car again until October 5 after qualifying twenty-fifth for the National 500 at Charlotte Motor Speedway in North Carolina. But he ran poorly and finished fourteenth, nine laps down. "After I came out of Atlanta with that second-place finish, I said, 'Man, we've got something going on here,'" Rusty recalls. "But everything went bad at the next race. And then it got worse. And that's when Roger said, 'This is something we don't need to do.' He thought it was really getting in the way of his Indy car effort."

Says Penske: "I had so many other programs I was doing, it was difficult to do an all-out attack on NASCAR. What I did was I gave him kind of a kick start. Rusty got some visibility. He picked it up from there."

Rusty made his final start in Penske's Caprice on October 5 in the National 500 Winston Cup race at Charlotte Motor Speedway. He finished fourteenth, nine laps down, as Dale Earnhardt drove to victory. Here he sits on pit road with Sterling Marlin to his outside and Marty Robbins behind Marlin. Cale Yarborough is behind Rusty. (David Chobat)

Between the runs with Penske, Rusty raced all across the Midwest and South. "I used to look at a book called the National Speedway Directory," he says. "It listed every track in the country. And I'd find a place and say to myself, 'I'm not racing at my regular places this weekend—maybe I'll go up there.' And I'd call these different tracks and see if they were racing, or try to get deal money to show up. By then I was winning a lot of races. And a promoter would sometimes say, 'Hey, if you come up here, I'll give you gas money and 500 bucks.' So I did that a lot."

Sometimes he would call Dick Trickle for advice. "How's the weather up there?" Rusty would ask, always getting around to other questions like, "What kinds of springs and shocks do you run at that track?"

The Evil Gang was still with Rusty. And all of them fondly remember their road trips. They would party after races, then pile four or five in a motel room and be up early the next morning, working on the car in the motel parking lot until they were chased off.

"One time we went to Salem, Indiana, to race," recalls Miller. "We all knew we had to drive all the way home after the race and go to work on Monday morning. And the Dog—Dave Wirz—was overserved after the race. He had way too many cocktails. So we loaded him in the back of the truck with the equipment and forgot all about him.

"Evidently, Dave came to about five o'clock in the morning when we were just coming close to St. Louis. There were no windows in the back, and it was darker than hell, and he didn't realize we were moving. So he got up, stumbled to the back, opened the door and started to get out. We were going about 70 miles per hour. Luckily, he hung onto the door while it slammed back and forth against the back of the truck. So we pulled off onto the side of the road to see what was wrong and found him hanging there. And we just laughed and laughed.

"Another time, we were coming back from Milwaukee. It was another one of those marathon deals. Everyone had been up all day and all night. And after we won the race, we all had a few beers. Of course, we had to drive back to St. Louis. And this guy in the front seat next to me was an engine man for Don Kirn named Tom. We called him "Terrible Tom." He'd had way too many beers.

"We were sitting there, and we had the sliding doors of the Hilton open. It was hot outside. We had an add-on air conditioner, but it didn't work. Nobody maintained it. So I'm driving along and it was the middle of the night and everybody was asleep in the two trucks we had. And I'm talking and not paying any attention to Tom. And he passed out. Well, he used to smoke like a fiend. And when he passed out, he dropped the cigarette on himself. The wind was coming through the truck. His shirt and jacket caught on fire. He was starting to burn up while sitting in his seat.

10/19/80 I-70

Two weeks after the Charlotte race, Rusty was at I-70 Speedway in Odessa, Missouri, for the World Cup 400 ASA season finale. He drove in the same uniform he had worn at Charlotte, where Gould and CAM2 motor oil had sponsored what turned out to be his final Winston Cup effort with Penske until they joined forces again in 1991. (Wallace collection)

Rusty was fast at I-70, but it didn't last. He finished eighteenth when he was forced to drop out of the race after 273 of 400 laps because his radiator failed. (Wallace collection)

"So I slapped him upside the head to wake him up. And when he woke up and saw that he was on fire, it scared him so bad, he threw up on himself and put the fire out. That was another one where we just had to stop and laugh."

Off the track, major developments were taking place in Rusty's life. On January 16, 1980, he and Patti were married. "I had seen her all the time at Lake Hill Speedway," Rusty says. "I remember when I first asked her to go out on a date. And she wanted to go. But, boy, that was a big deal to her parents. But we ended up going, and I've been with her ever since.

"We dated for five, six years, maybe longer. And so finally I said, 'Want to get married?' She said, 'OK.' So I told Charlie Chase about it, and of course he said, 'Let me handle it. I'll talk to my buddy at the courthouse.'"

The families didn't have enough money for both a big wedding and a big reception. "So we just went down to the courthouse and got married, and that night we had a hell of a party," Rusty says.

Rusty focused his primary effort in 1980 on the USAC series, but it did not have the same magic it had had in 1979. For one thing, Foyt was no longer racing in it. And although Rusty was leading the points in August, he eventually finished second to Joe Ruttman. Even more frustrating was USAC's efforts to put limits on Rusty's racing. The USAC stock car series was dying as the sanctioning body fought a bitter battle with CART for control of Indy car racing. Even so, USAC threatened to suspend its brightest star—Rusty—after he raced in certain ASA races that USAC considered in conflict with its own events. Miller became involved, writing letters to fend off their threats.

Rusty's greatest success in the 1980 USAC series came at Milwaukee, where he won both races. Including his 1979 victory, he had won three straight at the 1-mile flat oval. "Man, that Firebird I built just worked so good on those flat tracks," Rusty says. "It had a lot of grip."

Rusty continued his energetic pace in 1981 and 1982, bouncing from one track to the next, dabbling in this series and that. He was fast nearly everywhere he went. And he went everywhere. In February 1981, he was beaten by David Pearson in the Sportsman 300 at Daytona. In March he raced in Alabama. April found him in Ohio and Indiana, and as far east as Caraway Speedway in Asheboro, North Carolina. In May, he made his third Winston Cup start, racing the Number 98 Levi Garrett Pontiac in the World 600 at Charlotte for

By 1980, Mark Martin and Rusty had become two of the ASA's biggest stars, and they raced against each other at tracks all across the Midwest. Despite the intensity of their competition, they remained friends and occasionally traveled together. Here they talk between heat races at an unidentified track. (David Chobat)

Rusty and Patti (in chair) pose on their wedding day in 1980 with Rusty's best man, Charlie Chase and Patti's maid of honor, Mary Meyer. Patti says, "These two still remain our oldest and dearest friends." (Patti Wallace)

Johnny Rutherford, who was defending his 1980 Indianapolis 500 victory. Rusty tangled with Stan Barrett in the fourth turn on lap 205, crashed, and finished thirtieth. And just a few days after the 600, Rusty was back in Montgomery, Alabama, where he finished second to Butch Lindley, who raced a car Rusty had recently sold him. He raced at Cayuga International Speedway in Ontario, Canada, in late June, and won again at Milwaukee in July—his fourth victory in five USAC races there.

Although he ran well, Rusty did not win as often in 1981. He won no ASA or All-Pro races. His Milwaukee victory was his lone win in the USAC series. Perhaps the short-track racing had become old hat. In any event, his ambition was now aimed at the Winston Cup series. He had lost his foothold with Penske, but he was building his own car. In August, he again substituted for Rutherford at Talladega but finished twenty-first after his engine blew.

Rusty didn't have the money he needed to go Winston Cup racing, but he knew he could build a car—and get an engine from Don Kirn, and tires from John Childs, and help from the Evil Gang. So he took his own car to Charlotte in October of 1981. And he qualified nineteenth in the Child's Tire Number 72 Buick. Rusty lost three laps in 500 miles, but when the checkered flag fell, he was sixth, just ahead of Northern modified ace Geoff Bodine, who was also trying to get established in Winston Cup. It was Rusty's second top-ten finish in only five Cup races, and it gave him a tremendous boost.

In 1982 he entered the biggest NASCAR race of them all—the Daytona 500. He finished 10th in the first Twin 125 qualifying race and started nineteenth in his first 500. Rusty avoided the five-car crash that occurred when eventual race winner Bobby Allison's bumper fell off on the fourth lap. But on lap 41, Rusty's engine blew. He finished thirty-seventh.

The rotten luck continued after Daytona. Rusty qualified twenty-third for the Coca-Cola 500 at Atlanta on March 21 but blew another engine and finished thirty-fifth. He started twenty-third in a hot World 600 at Charlotte and completed three-fourths of NASCAR's longest race but crashed on lap 308 and finished twenty-ninth.

While Rusty fought for wisps of success in Winston Cup competition, his short-track results improved. For his All-Pro racing, Rusty had established a base in Gonzales, Louisiana, with car owner Nicky Prejean, whom he knew from his many trips to Alabama and Florida. Driving a Camaro, Rusty won four All-Pro races in 1982. He won at Macon, Georgia, in April and June, New Smyrna Speedway in Florida in July, and Birmingham, Alabama, in September.

And on October 3, Rusty ran away from a thirty-four-car ASA field in the Winchester 400 in Indiana. It was his first ASA victory since that first win back in Fort Wayne, Indiana, in 1978. And the winner's share of the purse—$9,800—was his biggest payday, according to *National Speed Sport News*.

Rusty took the money and promptly sank it back into his Number 72 Winston Cup Buick. He was returning to Daytona, come hell or high water. He avoided hell, but not high water. On the weekend of December 4 and 5, 1982, when Rusty was off in Florida racing in the Snowball Derby, the Meramec River spilled over its levees and flooded Valley Park.

"Whenever we get a flood around here in the Missouri or Mississippi rivers, it backs up into the Meramec, and Valley Park just goes under," says the *Post-Dispatch*'s John Sonderegger. "Rusty had this little bitty hole-in-the-wall garage in Valley Park, real close to the Meramec, and it was just covered."

"It was incredible," recalls Rusty. "We saw the water coming. And we started moving everything. We got all the welders and electrical stuff out of there before we went to Florida. But we didn't anticipate how high it would go. We thought it was only going to come up a couple of feet. So we stacked a bunch of concrete blocks and had that car 4 feet off the ground."

Rusty and Mark stand side by side during the driver's meeting before the Winston 100 NASCAR Grand American race at Mount Clemens Race Track in Michigan in June, 1981. Despite being competitive almost everywhere he raced Rusty never found victory lane in 1981. (David Allio)

Rusty made one Winston Cup start—his sixth—in the KangaROOs Buick Number 72 on November 8, 1981, at Atlanta International Raceway. He drove into the back of H.B. Bailey's car during the race, lost oil pressure, and finished twenty-ninth. (David Chobat)

Dragging this gas tank around Nashville Fairgrounds Speedway was not Rusty's only problem during the All American 400 on November 1, 1981. He finished seventeenth when a broken rear strut put him out of the event after 377 laps. (David Allio)

The floodwaters crested at more than 27 feet above flood stage. "They wouldn't even let you go down in Valley Park during the flood," Miller says. "I can remember standing on a hill with Charlie and Dog, looking out over the scene. You could just barely see the treetops."

"We had the car 4 feet off the ground, but the water came up 8 feet," Rusty says. "It went right over the roof of the car. It went over everything. It was the biggest mess you've ever seen in your life. All my pictures on the walls were sitting all crooked and full of mud. The carpet in our little office was wiped out. Everything was dripping and full of mud. Everything smelled. We had a balcony area 12 feet above the office, and I had it packed with stuff. Everything up there was OK.

"But my 1983 Daytona car was sitting there completely submerged because I didn't have it high enough off the ground. And when we went to Daytona, I remember coming off turn four with water coming out of the roll bars. I'm coming around this curve at close to 200 miles per hour and floodwater from the Meramec River is flying around the car. The water got in through all the pop rivet holes. I didn't know it was there. The car probably weighed about 20 pounds more because the roll cage was full of water."

Rusty's shop never fully recovered from the flood. After the water receded, the Evil Gang was too busy getting the car back in shape for Daytona to do anything beyond basic cleanup. Don Miller, meanwhile, was busy on another front. He had helped land Ramada Inns as a sponsor, then helped arrange a fund-raising campaign for the national Easter Seals Society.

"Wallace's Daytona 500 A Race To Help Others" read the headline in the February 2, 1983, edition of *National Speed Sport News*. Ramada Inns nationwide solicited pledges based on the number of miles Rusty completed in the 500.

"We're hoping to raise $100,000 to present to Pat Boone. He's the national Easter Seals chairman," Rusty told the paper. "The competition is definitely stiff, but I feel good. The car is handling a lot better this year."

As Speedweeks 1983 arrived, so did drenching rains. By Thursday, February 17, the day of the Twin 125 qualifying races, the infield was sodden. The day was overcast and threatening. In the first race, journeyman driver Bruce Jacobi lost control coming off turn two on lap 6. The car launched into a hideous series of flips, bouncing 30 feet into the air. Jacobi never regained consciousness and died four years later. More drivers crashed coming off turn two as the race continued.

Rusty started seventh in the second race. On lap 27, he was running tenth, leading a three-car pack. CBS cameras focused on them. "There's Richard Petty, going after Rusty Wallace in the 72 and the 62 car of Rick Wilson," CBS anchor Ken Squier said. A second later, as the camera switched back to the leaders, Wilson bumped Rusty's back bumper as the two cars sped off turn two.

Rusty drove this exotic late-model racer in the Snowball Derby, but "it just wasn't very good," he says. Here he pushes the car through the infield at Five Flags Speedway in Pensacola, Florida, before the race. (David Chobat)

After obtaining sponsorship from Ramada Inns and working for Easter Seals, Rusty was fourteenth fastest in Daytona qualifying. Here in his postqualifying portrait, he can barely contain his delight. Rusty is wearing the same red uniform that scared his little brother three days later when he crashed in the Twin 125s. (Charlie Chase collection)

Opposite: Rusty posted his second career top-ten finish in a Winston Cup race in his fifth event—the National 500 at Charlotte Motor Speedway on October 11. He started nineteenth in a Buick and finished sixth. (David Allio)

"We've got another terrible crash!" Squier shouted. Rusty's car tumbled through the backstretch grass, throwing rainwater and huge clumps of sodden grass high into the air. "A serious crash, again in turn two, has claimed another victim!" Squier said.

Rusty sat dazed in his car as rescue trucks slipped and slid through the muddy grass to reach him. He was smothered in muck and gasping for breath. When Rusty's car had spun, the windshield popped out. The car had lifted off the ground back end first and done a reverse flip, landing on the front of the roof, which dug deep into the wet ground and launched the car into a couple of hard forward rolls.

As the car's roof dug its huge divot, Rusty received the full force of the explosion of dirt, grass, and water through the open windshield. "He didn't have a full-face helmet at the time," Miller recalls. "And the sand and mud from the infield actually filled his mouth. He almost strangled to death. I grabbed Patti, and we went down to the infield care center. It looked like somebody had just dragged him through meat grinders."

"They were digging mud out of my mouth, and I remember I was choking on that stuff and spitting it out," Rusty says. "Somehow it got packed in my eyes and up my nose and ears. But the scary part was I was wearing a solid red uniform, and when Kenny came into the infield care center, he thought it was blood. He thought I was dead. He went nuts."

Recalls Kenny: "I remember being in the pits. The CBS hookups were behind us. I looked behind them and I saw his car flipping. And it scared me to death. And when I saw him, all I could see was dirt and sand and all this red all over Rusty. I thought all the red was blood. 'Oh, God,' I started crying. I thought it was over."

In a very real way, it was over. Rusty broke no bones in the crash, but he suffered a concussion and was badly bruised. He was taken to nearby Halifax Medical Center, where doctors painstakingly removed more mud and grit from his eyes. Considering the violence of the crash, he had survived in remarkably good shape.

But Rusty's spirit was devastated. His Winston Cup car—in which he had sunk all his extra money—was destroyed. His only choice was to haul his wrecked car back to his flood-ravaged shop in Valley Park and figure out what to do next.

"I do this for a living—that's all I do. I don't have a job to go to. I race and I race hard. I was willing to sell the socks off my grandmother's feet to keep going."

Although perhaps less speedy than the top Winston Cup crews, Rusty's ASA pit crew nonetheless threw everything they had into making his stops as quick as possible. As his car is being serviced, Rusty stares through the window net. (Don Miller collection)

Opposite: Rusty's first breakthrough came on April 17, 1983 at the season's third race at Atlanta, a fast track and one of Rusty's best. He averaged 151.622 MPH to beat Alan Kulwicki by a few car lengths. Here Rusty prepares to leave the pits as crew chief Paul Andrews (right) and Chris Hebler, who was with sponsor Ramada Inns, stand back. (Don Miller collection)

Rusty had hoped to impress a few Winston Cup car owners at Daytona, but he knew his flip down the backstretch hadn't impressed anyone. Car owners stay away from drivers who do that. He still wanted to get their attention, but now he had no Winston Cup car with which to do it.

"On the day of the crash, after Rusty overcame the shock of the whole thing, he was typical Rusty and bounced right back," Miller recalls. "But when he got back over to the track and saw how badly the car was wrecked, he was completely devastated. It had been a chance for us to move forward, especially with Ramada Inns. But this threw a monkey wrench into the whole deal. We had to transfer the Easter Seal pledge drive to another car that made the 500."

Battered, bruised, and demoralized, Rusty returned to St. Louis.

Miller told him: "You know, Rusty, what you may need to do is just go back and concentrate on one series and really kick some serious butt, and not try to race all over everywhere."

The USAC stock car series had deteriorated, so Rusty decided to set his sights on ASA. "I didn't have a Winston Cup car anymore," says Rusty. "My career was going to hell. I said, 'I'm not getting anything done here.' I decided to calm down and focus on one thing. I ran the whole ASA circuit in 1983 and ran for the championship. I had a brand-new Ray Dillon car. And me and Mark Martin and Dick Trickle battled all year."

The decision to run for the ASA championship did not stop Rusty from racing in other series. There were only twenty ASA races, which left plenty of time to race elsewhere. But he continued to have bad luck after the Daytona crash. The misfortune had actually started at the Snowball Derby the previous December. While his shop was being flooded in St. Louis, he was crashing out of the race in Florida.

The team's publicity photos were taken in the park at Valley Park, which only a few months earlier was under several feet of water. Here Rusty poses with Dave Wirz, crew chief Paul Andrews, and Steve Scheer, who joined the Evil Gang in its later years. (Don Miller collection)

Rusty and the other ASA drivers wave to the fans at Queen City Speedway in West Chester, Ohio, before a 300-lap race on May 22. Rusty led much of the race and at one point had an 8-second lead. But he dropped out on lap 255 with ignition failure and finished nineteenth. (Don Miller collection)

His first ASA race on February 27 brought more disappointment. Rusty had fought his way to second place late in a 100-lap event on a tiny quarter-mile flat track inside the Pontiac Silverdome, only to confront a spinning lapped car in the impossibly tight quarters. Trying to avoid it, Rusty ran into another car and flattened his right rear tire. He attempted to finish on the flat, but spun and finished 12th.

Rusty's luck finally changed when he returned to the All-Pro series for a 300-lap race at Alabama's half-mile Mobile International Speedway on March 27. He was back in his Nicky Prejean–owned, Southland Fire Equipment Camaro battling for a $100,000 purse that attracted many of the nation's finest short-track racers and even some Winston Cup stars. From the South came tough Freddy Fryar, Junior Niedecken, and Gary Balough. From the Midwest came Dick Trickle, Butch Miller, Mike Eddy, and Alan Kulwicki, who was then an ASA and ARTGO regular who had raced against Rusty in some USAC races. Donnie Allison came from Winston Cup. And Bobby Allison's oldest son, Davey, twenty-two, also was in the race.

Balough led the first third of the race but crashed on lap 106. Fryar led the next eighty-five laps but had tire problems and yielded the lead to Rusty. With only a handful of laps remaining, Rusty's transmission began to tighten up. The *G* forces apparently were pushing the gearbox oil to one side of the transmission, and all the parts weren't getting properly lubricated. But a caution flag flew. "With the slower speed, the fluid settled back to the bottom of the transmission, which saved me," Rusty told *National Speed Sport News* after the race. Rusty led the last eighty-one laps.

"I needed that win in the worst way," he said in victory lane. "I crashed in Pensacola and then had that bad one at Daytona. I do this for a living—that's all I do. I don't have

a job to go to. I race and I race hard. I was willing to sell the socks off my grandmother's feet to keep going."

Rusty enjoyed his trips South in those years. He was a regular visitor in Hueytown, Alabama, headquarters of the Allison clan and the "Alabama Gang." Rusty knew he could always stop at Bobby Allison's shop and work on his car. And he frequently did.

"Davey Allison would help," Rusty recalls. "Bobby would send Davey over to help me mount tires up, pull the spark plugs out, and help me get ready for the next race. He was my gofer. Clifford and Davey would always be around and would help out. They were just teenagers when I first got to know them."

"I was able to help people along the way," says Bobby Allison. "I really enjoyed that. And there were a few people, like Rusty, who seemed to really appreciate that help. He wanted to race. He was really an enthusiastic, energetic young driver who wanted to seek out anyone who could help him. So I just always regarded him as a special friend. I was sure that he could be very successful."

The season's second ASA race was at Nashville on April 10. Rusty was fast, and he opened a half-lap lead on Dick Trickle until his transmission locked up. He spun, hit the wall, and finished twenty-fifth. Rusty barely made it to the starting grid before the green flag fell for the next ASA race at Atlanta International Raceway on April 17. He had been fast in practice, but, as he told *NSSN*, "we were unhappy with the steering gear we had in

Rusty takes a rare moment of solitude to relax before the Coca-Cola 300 ASA race at Lonesome Pine International Raceway in Coeburn, Virginia, on June 11, 1983. Rusty led the first 58 laps but retired with ignition failure on lap 209 and finished seventeenth. (David Allio)

The ASA field was lined up and the crew chiefs had signaled that they were ready to go in this 1983 race. Dick Trickle in the Number 99 car was on the pole for this event. Paul Andrews stands behind Rusty's car. (Don Miller collection)

The second of Rusty's three ASA victories in 1983 came at Toledo Speedway in Ohio on June 4. Here he celebrates at the finish line following the 300-lap race. (Don Miller collection)

the car during Saturday practice, and had to fly a new unit in overnight, then change it [race] morning. We had to reset the front end and almost didn't get it done in time."

Fifteen minutes before the command to start engines, Rusty and the crew were still hurriedly making the final adjustments. With 8 minutes to go, they finally pushed Rusty's Camaro to the line. The repairs worked. Rusty and Alan Kulwicki engaged in a drafting duel that lasted almost all 200 miles. Rusty beat Kulwicki by three-tenths of a second, averaging 151.622 MPH. Lap averages under the green flag reached 171 MPH, 3 MPH quicker than Kulwicki's pole speed.

Rusty won again on April 23 in Mississippi, leading 91 laps of a 200-lap All-Pro race at Jackson International Speedway. But he finished second to Dick Trickle in a 150-mile ASA race at Milwaukee on May 1, then lost to him again in a 200-lap All-Pro race in Montgomery, Alabama, on May 7. "Veteran track observers called it the best race ever held at the track," *NSSN* reported. The two drivers had battled furiously until Trickle lost a lap with a bad pit stop. He made up the lap with twenty-six remaining, then came all the way around and passed Rusty for the lead with just three laps left. Afterward Rusty sat dejectedly on the pit wall and told *NSSN:* "You can never count the world's winningest short-track driver out of a race until the checkered flag falls."

On May 22, Rusty led most of the ASA race at Queen City Speedway in West Chester, Ohio, but fell out on lap 255 of 300 with ignition failure. He finished nineteenth. The series moved upstate on June 4 to Toledo Speedway, where Rusty whipped the field in a 300-lap race despite receiving serious body damage in a collision with a lapped car on lap 38. Rusty's car did not handle well right after the crash, but his crew

"When she started sliding toward pit wall, you can't imagine what went through my mind... All I could think about was all the work it took to get to that point, and it looked like it was going right out the window."

pounded the bent sheet metal and fixed the spoiler during yellow-flag pit stops. Rusty led the final 124 laps, but not without pressure. His radio broke midway through the race, so his crew was unable to tell him that Mark Martin was many laps down when Martin appeared in his mirror, eager to pass.

"Man, you just never count the Kid out," Rusty said afterward. "And my radio was out, so I figured I'd better not take a chance. We had a lot of fun, but I would have let him go if I'd known the situation."

Heading into the June 18 ASA race at Berlin Speedway in Marne, Michigan, Rusty was third in championship points, trailing Dick Trickle and Bobby Dotter. But engine failures during warm-ups at Berlin left him without a car. As happens so often in racing, another competitor came to the rescue. A part-time ASA competitor, Dave Tomczak, lent Rusty his car, and Rusty managed to finish eighth.

Rusty made sure he was better prepared when the ASA series arrived in Milwaukee for the Miller High Life 200 race on July 10. He had been involved in a big crash in an ASA race the week before at Bristol International Raceway in Tennessee but had recovered to finish fifth. Now he trailed only Trickle in ASA points.

So Rusty took no chances. He carried two cars to Milwaukee. The precaution, as it turned out, allowed Rusty to display the same generosity to Dick Trickle that Tomczak had shown Rusty. The reason? Trickle came to Milwaukee without a car.

Trickle had returned to his Wisconsin home after the Bristol race to learn that his chassis sponsor, the Canadian driver Junior Hanley, had demanded his chassis back. Two weeks earlier, Trickle and Hanley had been battling for the lead at the end of a race at Cayuga in Ontario. They touched. Hanley spun. Trickle won. And now Trickle was without a car.

NSSN reported: "In an outstanding gesture of sportsmanship, Trickle's main challenger in ASA competition, Rusty Wallace, and car owner Nicky Prejean offered their Dillon backup machine to Trickle for the points-rich event in which Trickle was defending champion." But both cars had mechanical problems in the race. Rusty finished eighteenth. Trickle was twenty-fourth. Alan Kulwicki won.

Rusty finished fifth in the Molson 300 ASA race in Ontario, Canada, on July 31. And at Anderson, Indiana, on August 6, he was on his way to victory until a slower car spun in front of him late in the race. Rusty hesitated enough to let Bob Senneker by

Rusty's Camaro shows crash damage—and the team's previous efforts to repair it—during a pit stop at Wisconsin State Fair Park Speedway in Milwaukee on July 10. Although Milwaukee was one of Rusty's best tracks, he finished eighteenth, five laps down, in this race. (Don Miller collection)

for the win. But Rusty's second-place finish gave him the points lead.

It was now mid-August. The ASA season was down to its final seven races. Rusty was racing for points, not victories. And he was doing it well. He finished fifth at Lonesome Pine International Raceway in Coeburn, Virginia. He finished eighth in the ASA's return to Berlin Raceway and was seventh in a race at the Minnesota State Fair on September 5. With four races to go, Rusty held a slim 37-point lead over Trickle.

But Rusty's car was fast right off the trailer for the 150-mile ASA race at Michigan International Speedway on September 18. He won the pole and discovered that he could drive his car anywhere in Michigan's wide turns. After leading the first twenty-five laps, Rusty suddenly veered onto pit road. His engine was overheating. Debris covered the radiator grille.

Rusty charged back and was in the lead again by lap 48. He led the final twenty-seven laps, beat Trickle by eight tenths of a second, and increased his championship lead ever so slightly to fifty-three points. Two races later, after finishing tenth at Winchester and fourth at Indianapolis Raceway Park, Rusty led Trickle by seventy points.

The season finale was an ASA All-Pro shoot-out called the All American 400 at Nashville International Raceway, and 14,000 fans packed the grandstands to see the Sunday afternoon battle on the 0.596-mile banked track. To win the ASA title, Rusty had to finish within sixteen positions of Trickle.

Rusty appeared ready to beat Trickle and everyone else when he won the pole. He led the first fifty-eight laps. But he began to fall back. A right rear tire was slowly going down. He was lapped by leader Jim Sauter on lap 70. When Rusty finally came in under the green flag on lap 83, he entered the pits too quickly—considering one tire was flat—lost control, and skidded into the pit wall. The collision damaged the nose of the car. The team had no choice but to hold him in the pits and fix it.

"When she started sliding toward pit wall, you can't imagine what went through my mind," Rusty said afterward. "All I could think about was all the work it took to get to that point, and it looked like it was going right out the window." Fortunately for

The racing was hard and tight at the WDGY 300 at the Minnesota State Fairgrounds Speedway in St. Paul on September 5. As Ed Howe leads the pack, Rusty battles on the outside of a three-wide group that includes Jay Sauter and Kent Stauffer. Mike Eddy trails in the Number 88 car. Rusty eventually finished seventh, three laps down. (Don Miller collection)

Here Rusty drives to the inside of Bob Senneker at Michigan. Senneker was challenging for the lead on lap 65 when he spun in turn two and backed hard into the wall. Rusty's victory at Michigan was his third ASA win of the season and gave him a sweep of the two ASA races on superspeedways. (Don Miller collection)

This shot of Rusty at speed was taken from the second turn at Winchester. It freezes his Camaro and reveals a considerable amount of debris covering the grille of his car. The car began to overheat, and Rusty had to go to the pits. (Don Miller collection)

In this dramatic photograph from the 1983 season, Rusty leads the pack heading through the first and second turns of an ASA short track. Alan Kulwicki trails in the Number 97 car, followed by Dick Trickle. (Don Miller collection)

"This was the first salary Rusty Wallace made in racing," Miller says. "The last time he had had a salary was when he was working at the vacuum cleaner company with his uncle."

Rusty, the attrition rate had been high, and although he finished seven laps down, it was still good enough for eleventh place—and the American Speed Association 1983 championship. Rusty beat Trickle by only twenty-three points. But he had won three races. He had posted fourteen top tens. He had earned the title.

Rusty's performance did not go unnoticed among Winston Cup owners. One of them, Cliff Stewart, a car owner who had been involved in NASCAR racing since 1963, called him.

"When the telephone call came, I wasn't there," Rusty says. "I was off racing again in the Snowball Derby. Cliff Stewart couldn't find me. And I always considered it a huge blessing that he didn't."

Stewart was a blunt-spoken furniture dealer from Thomasville, North Carolina. Twenty-two drivers had driven his cars during his three decades in NASCAR, including Joe Weatherly, Jim Paschal, Jimmy Pardue, Bob Welborn, Tiny Lund, and, most recently, Geoff Bodine.

But Stewart had fired Bodine with two races remaining in the 1983 season after Bodine told him he was moving to another team in 1984. Stewart wanted Rusty to fill in. When Stewart couldn't find him, he turned to Donnie Allison. Allison had terrible luck in Stewart's car. He blew an engine and finished thirty-sixth at Atlanta, and was fourteenth at California's Riverside, two laps down.

Allison's tepid results again opened the door for Rusty. In late November, Stewart finally reached him. Stewart said his son, Howard, had been watching Rusty. "He says you're the guy I need to drive my car and work with this team," Stewart said.

Recalls Miller: "Stewart was really a self-made man. He was a crusty old guy—enjoyable, but nevertheless crusty. I flew down to his place, Spectrum Furniture in Thomasville, to talk with him on November 30, 1983. I can still remember it. He was sitting on the other side of the desk with his foot up on one edge of the desk, smoking a cigar, and expounding on the benefits of being with Stewart Racing.

"He told me, 'You know what was wrong with Bodine?'

"I said, 'No, I don't, Mr. Stewart.'

The Winchester 400 at fast, tough Winchester Speedway in Indiana on October 2 was the eighteenth of twenty races in the ASA season. Rusty came into the event with 1,636 points for the season. Dick Trickle had 1,599 points. Here Rusty flies through the high-banked, rough turns. (Don Miller collection)

At the ASA banquet, Rusty accepts the trophy as 1983 champion. He had won his first major series title on the strength of three victories and fourteen top-ten finishes, beating Dick Trickle by a mere twenty-three points in the end. (Don Miller collection)

Opposite: In the pits at Winchester, with valuable time passing, Rusty looks toward the scoreboard as Paul Andrews and the crew work feverishly to fix the problem and cool the car. Rusty completed 363 laps and finished tenth. But Trickle did even worse, and Rusty's championship lead grew to seventy-eight points over Trickle. (Don Miller collection)

"And he said, 'He wore one of those closed helmets. We figured out he just never got enough oxygen.'

"Of course, I agreed with him—anything to get the ride for 1984. I remember telling him, 'This kid has no money, so we can't go in on a deal where he's driving only for percentages of the purse.' They agreed that Rusty would receive an annual salary of $40,000 plus expenses and 35 percent of his race winnings. "This was the first salary Rusty Wallace made in racing," Miller says. "The last time he had had a salary was when he was working at the vacuum cleaner company with his uncle."

On December 7, Miller flew back to North Carolina, this time with Rusty, and they signed a contract. The excitement was heightened because Stewart had landed a major sponsor—Gatorade.

"They gave me a Gatorade coat," Rusty says. "I was so proud of that thing. I wore it everywhere. I went to the ASA championship banquet wearing that old green Gatorade coat. Everybody else was in tuxes and evening gowns, and I was walking around in that Gatorade coat."

But the new job meant Rusty and Patti would have to move to North Carolina. As often as Rusty had roamed the country to race, he had always lived in Missouri, mostly in St. Louis. Patti had as well. Plus, they now had a three-year-old. Greg was born on January 24, 1980. Rusty's new opportunity was exciting, but it was daunting. They left with $3,000—their life savings.

"I closed up my little shop, which was still half under mud, and got ready to go," Rusty recalls. "Cliff sent an old van up to St. Louis, and we loaded all our stuff in the van. Then Patti and I loaded Greg up and we left home. And that was as scared as I've ever been in my life."

Recalls Kenny: "Me and my wife were in a truck, and Rusty and Patti were in a car. And we left St. Louis together and drove to North Carolina. We followed each other bumper to bumper. When we got to Statesville, I made a right on Interstate 77. And I went on down to Charlotte and became a crewman on the Levi Garrett team. And Rusty kept going straight on Interstate 40 to High Point to drive for Cliff Stewart."

"As we got close to High Point," Rusty says, "we stayed in an old Econolodge for nineteen bucks a night—just Patti and I and Greg. Then Cliff let us stay at this old house he had. The first thing I did when I walked in the house was I went to take a shower. I picked up a towel, and mice came running out. We were scared. We were nervous. It was the first time we had been away from home. And I kept saying, 'We'll make it. This is our big break.' And that's how it started."

9 Becoming a Contender

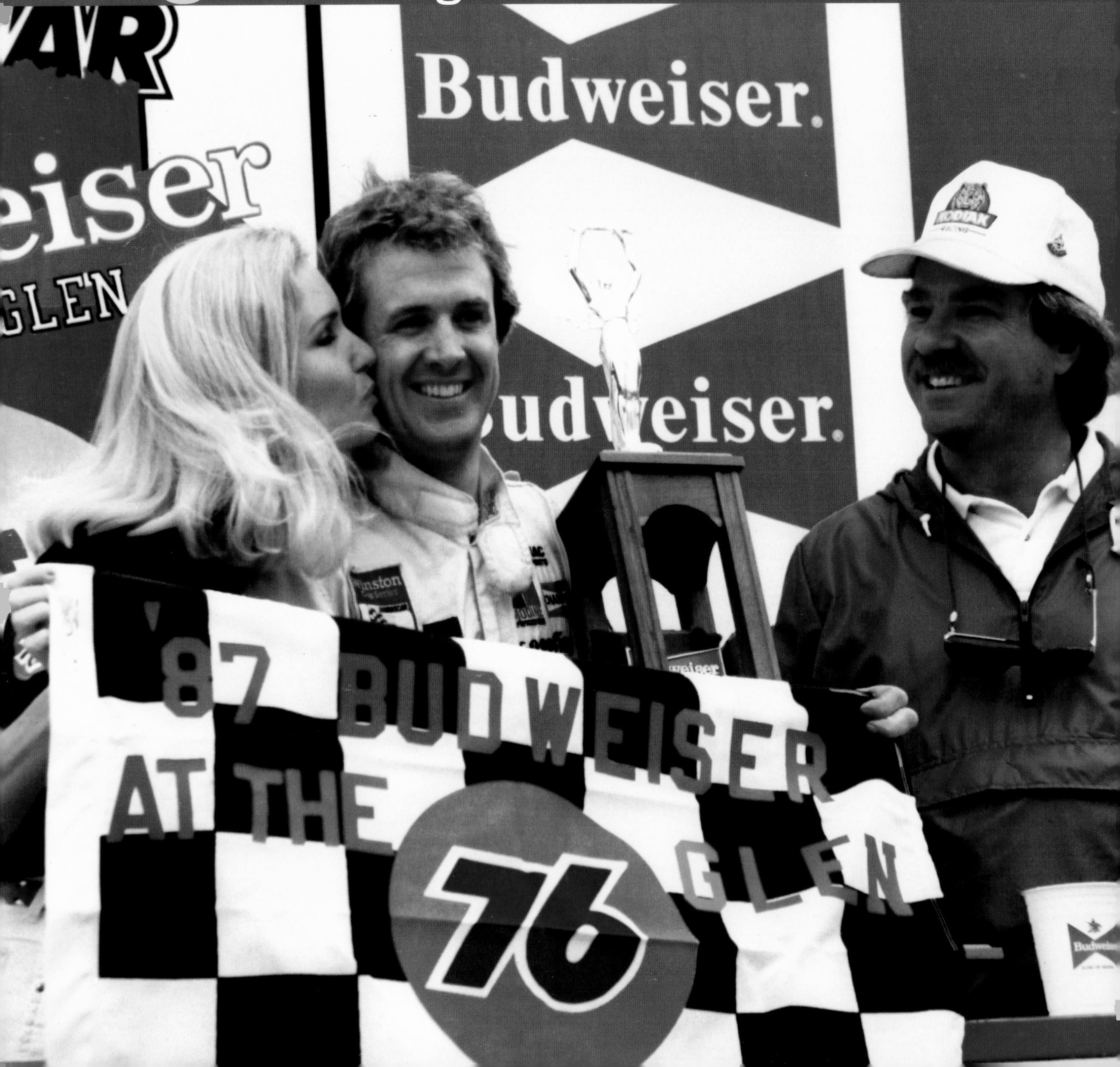

"That first year was terrible....We blew up and crashed, blew up and crashed, blew up and crashed."

On lap 372 at Rockingham, Rusty got caught up in a wreck with Lennie Pond, Harry Gant, and Tim Richmond. Rusty hit the wall hard, and it took more than half an hour for the track officials to repair the damage to the wall. (Bryan Hallman)

Opposite: Rusty's victory at Watkins Glen was his first win of the 1987 season. He took the lead with twenty-eight laps to go and won by 11.8 seconds over Terry Labonte. Here in victory lane, he gets a kiss from the Unocal trophy girl while car owner Raymond Beadle looks on. (David Chobat)

As difficult as it was for Rusty and Patti to pick up roots and move to North Carolina, Don Miller saw an unforgettable sense of determination from within Rusty before the 1984 season started.

"He told me, 'I'm going to do this, Don, and it's going to be hard, but I'm going to do it because I can do it.' It was amazing," Miller says, "It was like, 'This is my destiny, and I'm going to fulfill it.'"

But Rusty's spirit did not excuse him from paying his dues. He started twenty-seventh in his second Daytona 500 but crashed on lap 98 and finished thirtieth. Things improved, at least for a moment, when he qualified fifth at Richmond. But he finished sixteenth, four laps down. He crashed at Rockingham, broke a water pump at Atlanta, blew an engine at North Wilkesboro, crashed with four other cars at Darlington, lost his steering at Talladega. The list seemed endless.

"That first year was terrible," Rusty recalls. "We blew up and crashed, blew up and crashed, blew up and crashed. And we lost Gatorade at the end of the year."

It could have been worse. Rusty finished sixth at Pocono, fourth in the Southern 500, and fifth at North Carolina's North Wilkesboro. He was fourteenth in Winston Cup points. And he was the 1984 NASCAR Winston Cup rookie of the year.

"He ran fairly well," Miller recalls. "He had a period of adjustment with the crew chief, Darrell Bryant. He was a real old-school crew chief. And he really taught Rusty how not to be so aggressive. Rusty was so fired up—he had such an aggressive driving style— he was a lot stronger and had a lot greater gift for propelling that vehicle than the vehicle had to give back. He was a lot faster than the car.

Rusty started twenty-seventh in the 1984 Daytona 500—his first race for team owner Cliff Stewart in the Number 88 Gatorade Pontiac. He crashed on lap ninety-eight and finished thirtieth. (Don Miller collection)

"And I kept telling him: 'You're a Yankee, and you're going to have a certain critical eye cast on you. The worst thing we can do right now is get these people upset. You've got to keep pushing the envelope but not tearing the sides out. And he made a major adjustment. You could see it. He really adjusted his driving style more to the capabilities of the car than to his own abilities."

The 1985 season got off to a much better start. Rusty finished eighth in the Daytona 500 and posted five top-ten finishes in the first eight races. At Bristol on April 6, Rusty led his first Winston Cup green flag laps. He took the lead from Dale Earnhardt on lap 138 and led until lap 147, when Earnhardt passed him again. Rusty also led laps 205 through 222 before finishing fifth.

But engine failures took a heavy toll. Rusty failed to finish a dozen races, ten because of blown engines. He finished nineteenth in points.

"About two-thirds of the way through the 1984 season, Cliff decided to start his own engine program," Miller recalls. "And in 1985, the engines just weren't hanging together. Cliff was blaming a lot of the problems that the car was having on Rusty. I wasn't buying that. The engines were blowing up one right after another. And there was a lot of unrest in the team. I knew we were going to have to look around for something to make it better or move on."

When Stewart came down hard on Rusty in a newspaper article, Miller and Rusty knew it was time to look for another ride. But Rusty was already being scouted.

"We were running good enough that we kept catching the eyes of Barry Dodson and Harold Elliott, the crew chief and engine builder for Raymond Beadle," Rusty says.

Dodson had started in Winston Cup with Richard Petty. "I had kept my eye on Rusty all through the years," he says, "and I knew of the success he had in ASA. I watched him work on his own stuff, doing his own car preparation. And I thought then, and I think now, that working on your own car is a key to being successful. We knew we wanted him. We didn't know if we could get him. But Harold and I felt like if we could get together with him, maybe we could set the world on fire."

Beadle owned the Blue Max Racing team and the Old Milwaukee Pontiac driven by Tim Richmond in 1985. Beadle and Miller were old acquaintances from the drag racing circuit. Rusty had good rapport with Pontiac. The team seemed young, eager, and talented. "I went to Dallas late in the season and talked to Raymond at his drag racing shop," Miller says. "He was only going to run fifteen races in 1986. But I said we had a sponsor from the ASA car, Alugard, that we could bring over. Raymond still really didn't have any money to go forward with. When he had Tim Richmond, all those moneys went with Richmond when he switched over to drive for Rick Hendrick."

Undaunted by the prospect of not running a full season, Rusty and the team quickly realized they could make magic together. He finished eighth in the Daytona 500. He was tenth at Richmond, twelfth at North Carolina's Rockingham, and eighth at Atlanta.

"The idea was to run the first three or four races and take a break," Miller says. "Rusty ran so well, everyone said, 'Let's not take a break. Let's go on and do some of the short track races.' The tracks were close by. It wouldn't cost as much. Rusty was always good on the short tracks. So we decided to do it. We'd figure out a way to pay for it, somehow, some way."

Bristol came first—the fifth race of the season. "Rusty qualified pretty well [fourteenth], but he said, 'I can win this race,'" Miller recalls. "I was back in St. Louis. And he called and said, 'You've gotta watch this race Sunday. I can win this race.'"

Neil Bonnett led the first seventy-four laps but crashed. Dale Earnhardt took over in front. But Rusty's Pontiac was getting stronger. On lap 240, he took the lead from Terry Labonte. He led again from lap 310 to 314 and finally took the lead for good on lap 400.

"He got up to the front once but fell back after a bad pit stop," Miller says. "Then he got up front again. And fell back again. When he got up front the third time, he stayed there."

Patti Wallace took this snap shot of Rusty talking with Ricky Rudd before qualifying at Martinsville on April 28. Rusty, Patti, and their son Greg moved from St. Louis to North Carolina before the season to commit to driving full-time in Winston Cup, but the early results were disappointing. Rusty finished fifteenth in the race the next day. (Patti Wallace)

In victory lane, after leading 174 laps of one of the most physically demanding races on the schedule, Rusty was half out of breath, but not out of words. "It was the dream of a lifetime," he said. "It was just something I didn't think would ever happen, because I worked so hard. . . . That last 30 laps seemed like 200. I just kept driving every line as carefully as I could. Fifty laps left in the race, I said, 'Boy, I wish there was just one more lap left.' And then that one lap came, and I said, 'Thank God.'"

Rusty's first career Winston Cup victory was also Dodson's first. "Some people doubted Rusty's ability," Dodson told reporters. "Some people doubted he'd ever make it big. Well, he made it big today. Mark this date."

Recalls Miller: "All of a sudden, this kid from St. Louis, supposedly a marginal driver, becomes a superhero overnight. I mean *overnight*. We started getting calls. Raymond started getting calls. People started to come to us. It was really the beginning of Rusty's souvenir business. It fueled Rusty's popularity and really got him into the forefront in terms of recognition. And as the season wore on, he built his confidence. And he built not only his personal confidence, but he built his confidence in that group of guys he worked with. And the team gained confidence in him. They took this unknown driver and, by developing a relationship, started to win. And pretty soon they started to go to every race thinking they were going to win."

Rusty had a strong summer in 1986, posting six top-ten finishes in nine races from late May to mid-August. And at Virginia's Martinsville in September, he won again after beating Geoff Bodine out of the pits during the last yellow flag. He finished the 1986 season with his best record yet. He won his first two races, had sixteen top-ten finishes, and collected more than $500,000 in prize money. He finished sixth in points. And he and his team had done all this on a severely constricted budget.

"Raymond ran the whole 1986 season damn near out of his pocket," Rusty says. "Alugard was only giving us $200,000, and even back then it was costing a million dollars a year to run the full season."

Says Dodson: "We were starting to get a glimpse of what Rusty could do. He had won our fifth time out in Bristol. And he had done it again at Martinsville. Rusty had no hobbies. He didn't care about baseball, basketball, bowling, or golf. He lived, ate, and breathed racing. To have a guy that cared nothing about anything but racing fueled the fire in the rest of the team. The guys thought, 'Gee, this guy really wants it bad. He's

Rusty's Blue Max crew gasses his Pontiac during a pit stop in the 1986 Daytona 500. At the front of the car, crew chief Barry Dodson tapes the radiator grille to add speed by improving the car's efficiency in cutting through the wind. (Brian Cleary)

Opposite: With smoke pouring out from his Gatorade Pontiac, Rusty heads to the pits at Talladega after crashing in the 1984 Winston 500. Rusty started thirty-first and finished thirty-first after calling it a day on lap 107 when his steering failed. (David Chobat)

"I had twelve laps to go and a 9-second lead over Kyle Petty, and that's like half a lap, and I dropped a cylinder and fell out. We just had crazy little problems that put me out of the winner's circle."

hungry.' I think he was the missing piece of the puzzle. Rusty got us to where we needed to be—a solid contender week in and week out."

Beadle found a new sponsor, Kodiak, for 1987. That guaranteed the level of funding that the team needed to make a well-rounded, competitive effort. Rusty had been paid $70,000 plus 40 percent of the prize money in 1986, which was $222,941. For 1987, he received a raise to $100,000. (His 40 percent of the 1987 prize money ended up being $276,260).

Rusty won two more races in 1987—Watkins Glen in New York and Riverside. He had nine top-five finishes and sixteen top-tens. He finished fifth in Winston Cup points. But it was a season with a lot of could-have-beens. "We felt we could have won six or seven races," he told reporters at the end of the year. "We were leading at the end of some races when crazy little things would go wrong, like a cracked oil pan or something. One was the Coca-Cola 600, where I had twelve laps to go and a 9-second lead over Kyle Petty, and that's like half a lap, and I dropped a cylinder and fell out. We just had crazy little problems that put me out of the winner's circle. If we didn't have those problems, we could have won the championship, and a lot of races."

Still, it had been an encouraging year. Dodson was particularly satisfied by the victory at Watkins Glen. "We had run about five laps after a pit stop," he recalls. "Rusty radios in and says he has a flat right-front tire. So I say, 'OK, pit.' And I call for four tires. I can see guys on the Levi Garrett crew laughing and pointing to the tires because I changed all four tires, and it was obviously the right front tire that was flat. So Rusty leaves and gets halfway up through the esses and comes back on the radio and asks, 'Any reason why we changed four tires?'

"'Yeah,' I told him. 'We're in good shape for the rest of the race now, and we really didn't lose much more ground.'"

With twenty-eight laps to go, a yellow flag flew, and Dodson hit the jackpot with his strategy. "We don't need tires! We don't need tires!" Rusty hollered as he came down pit road. Dodson thought, "No kidding." After a fuel-only pit stop, Rusty left the pits first and took the lead.

An unidentified crewman talks with Rusty after the 1985 TranSouth 500 at Darlington Raceway. Despite the damage, Rusty finished fifth, two laps down. It was his second straight fifth-place finish, but it was also his last top-five finish in a season that would become plagued with engine failures. (Bryan Hallman)

"It was really gratifying, the picture-perfect way it fell," Dodson says. "But it was going to be close on fuel. And right behind us was Terry Labonte in that Junior Johnson Chevrolet. Tim Brewer was in charge there, and that car . . . well, let's just say it had a pretty big fuel cell. I *knew* Terry would be able to make it. So I told Rusty to run the car as hard as it would go when the green flag dropped so we could get all the cushion we could. As he was coming down the backstretch on his way to taking the white flag, the fuel light came on. Rusty dove onto pit road and we took the white flag on pit road. As soon as we got some fuel in, Rusty tried to take off. The car stalled, then it lit up and he took off like John Force. Back then there was no pit road speed. And I called Red Dog [Brian Barnes], who was over in the esses, and said, 'Do you see him yet?' And Red Dog replied: 'He went by here like a bat out of hell.' " Rusty beat Labonte by 11.8 seconds.

Rusty races inside Dale Earnhardt in a side-by-side duel during the 1986 Daytona 500. He was now racing Raymond Beadle's Pontiac and had brought the Alugard sponsorship with him. He finished one lap down and was eighth in the 500 for the second straight year. (Brian Cleary)

Although the Winston Cup season ended poorly, Rusty went to victory lane the day before the season finale in the 1984 Atlanta All American Challenge Twin 100s for late-model sportsman cars. He emerges from his car in victory lane as Ned Jarrett (at right) prepares to conduct the winner's interview. (Don Miller collection)

As the 1988 season started, Rusty and his crew believed their time had come. Rusty finished seventh in the Daytona 500, his highest finish ever. He was seventh at Richmond. He ran second to Dale Earnhardt at Atlanta, then posted a pair of fourth-place finishes at Bristol and North Wilkesboro.

When the series went to Southern California for the Budweiser 400 at Riverside International Raceway on June 12, Rusty had posted three straight top-ten finishes and

was only sixteen points behind Dale Earnhardt for the Winston Cup points lead. Rusty qualified second at Riverside and ran well throughout the race. With fourteen laps to go, he took the lead from Neil Bonnett. Terry Labonte chased him on the last lap, but Rusty won by three-tenths of a second. The victory was his

Although Rusty was exhausted during the final 50 laps of his first Winston Cup victory at Bristol International Raceway, he quickly revived for the postrace ceremonies, which included the trophy presentation and a dance on the hood of his car as his Blue Max crew cheered him on. Rusty led the final 101 laps and pulled away to a whopping 10.69-second victory over Ricky Rudd, which is more than half a lap at Bristol. (David Chobat)

Crew chief Barry Dodson unloads on Rusty in victory lane at Riverside International Raceway after his win at the 1987 Winston Western 500. Rusty took the lead with eleven laps to go after front-runner Geoff Bodine got a flat tire. It gave Rusty a sweep of the two 1987 Winston Cup road races. (David Chobat)

third straight on a road course, and it cemented his reputation as NASCAR's best road racer. And for the first time in his career, Rusty Wallace was leading the Winston Cup championship, even if it was only by four points.

But the 1988 season was shrouded by the dark specter of the Goodyear-Hoosier tire war. As the two tire makers battled for supremacy, they built ever softer, faster tires. Reliability suffered. Buddy Baker and Harry Gant were hurt at Charlotte after wicked crashes following tire failures. At Pocono, Bobby Allison was gravely injured in a career-ending crash after his tire apparently went down. He crashed and was T-boned by Jocko Maggiacomo.

Rusty was shaken but undeterred. He finished third at Pocono. And at Michigan on June 26, he won his first superspeedway race, surviving a furious challenge by Bill Elliott, and crossed the finish line only 0.28 seconds ahead. "It's special to win my first [superspeedway] race here because this track is owned by Roger Penske," Rusty said afterward. "He was the man who gave me my first break in Winston Cup racing."

The season was now half-finished, and Rusty had a 140-point lead over Earnhardt. But Elliott loomed in third, only 150 points back. And after Elliott won two in a row at Daytona and Pocono, he was only three points behind Rusty.

At Talladega, ten cars battled furiously to the checkered flag in the DieHard 500. It was one of the wildest last laps Rusty had ever experienced. "We wrecked for a solid lap and got away with it," he said. Rusty was fifth. Elliott finished ninth. And when Rusty finished second and Elliott third at both Watkins Glen and Michigan, it began to appear as if it would be a two-man battle for the championship down the homestretch.

Watkins Glen featured a great finish as Rusty caught Ricky Rudd on the last lap and beat on his bumper in an unsuccessful attempt to get by. At Michigan, Rusty rebounded from a broken oil line and a cracked header to finish second, 4 seconds behind Davey Allison. Heading to Bristol and the final ten races, he was only twenty-one points ahead of Elliott. It was no time for trouble.

But trouble was exactly what he found at Bristol. And it dealt a crippling blow to his title hopes. The tire war had been claiming cars and drivers all year. Now it was Rusty's turn. At 2:05 p.m. on Friday, August 26, a right front tire blew

When this portrait was taken in the garage at Talladega Superspeedway in May 1986, Rusty had his first victory under his belt and was primed for more. But it didn't happen that weekend. He finished thirteenth in the Winston 500. In the background is Terry Labonte's Number 44 Piedmont Airlines Oldsmobile. (Elmer Kappell)

In a fantastic finish, Rusty holds off Darrell Waltrip by a car length to win the 1988 Oakwood Homes 500 at Charlotte. Waltrip tried every move he could to pass Rusty in the final two laps, to no avail. "That was the wildest Pontiac I've ever followed," Waltrip said afterward. Said Rusty: "On the last lap, he pushed me all the way down the backstretch and into the third turn." (David Chobat)

on Rusty's Pontiac as it sped through the fourth turn. The car went straight into the outside wall. And when it bounced off, the right front wheel dug into the pavement and launched the car into barrel rolls down the front stretch. The car flipped at least five times, coming down hard on the asphalt each time. It finally came to a stop right side up, half on the pit wall.

ESPN pit reporter Dr. Jerry Punch, who doubled as a trauma surgeon in a Florida hospital emergency room, was one of the first on the scene. Rusty was unconscious and wasn't breathing. Punch resuscitated him. Rescuers cut the roll bar and carefully lifted Rusty from his seat, a neck brace placed securely around his neck. Rusty spent the night at Bristol Memorial Hospital, but other than severe bruises and a big headache, he was not seriously injured.

"Jerry Punch was right there, and if he hadn't been, I'm afraid there would have been some damage done," says Judy. "I sent him a thank you letter."

After the crash, the crew did major surgery to prepare another car. Their backup was a show car that had spent the previous few months sitting in malls. They cannibalized the wrecked car and threw together another race car. Rusty managed to drive a few laps during the race two days later, then turned the wheel over to a relief driver, Larry Pearson, who avoided trouble and finished ninth, seven laps down. But Elliott finished second and took over the lead by sixteen points.

Rusty and Elliott again battled head-to-head in the Southern 500 at South Carolina's Darlington Raceway. Elliott prevailed, beating Rusty by just a couple of car lengths.

Richmond, which had been one of Rusty's best tracks, became his Waterloo in the battle for the championship. Just before the race—the first on the new three-quarter-

"I think we have the number-one team, and I'm driving like it's number one. If we lose the championship, it will be very disheartening. Even if we do lose, I will feel like we've won it."

mile oval—Rusty and other drivers elected to switch from Hoosier tires to Goodyears. Because it came after qualifying, the switch meant they had to start at the back of the pack. On the first lap, Richard Petty and Lake Speed tangled. As the field slowed, Geoff Bodine slammed into the back of Rusty's Pontiac and literally drove over it, inflicting massive damage to both cars, particularly Rusty's. He lasted only seventeen laps and finished thirty-fifth in the thirty-six-car field. Rusty fell to third in the championship race, 2 points behind Earnhardt and 119 behind Elliott.

At Dover, Delaware, the race became a battle among the three points leaders. Elliott won, capturing his sixth race of the season. Earnhardt was second. Rusty finished third. But when Earnhardt stumbled at Martinsville and Rusty finished third, he vaulted past Earnhardt into second in the championship battle. With five races remaining, Rusty trailed Elliott by 124 points.

Thus started one of the great charges in Winston Cup history. At Charlotte, Rusty lost two laps while the crew changed a malfunctioning carburetor. He made up both laps, passed Brett Bodine for the lead with twelve laps to go, and held off Darrell Waltrip in a furious, bumper-banging battle on the last lap.

Rusty and Dale Earnhardt race side by side in the 1988 Southern 500 at Darlington Raceway. The race became a three-car show featuring Rusty, Earnhardt, and Bill Elliott, who won by 0.24 seconds. Rusty was second, with Earnhardt on his bumper. (Bryan Hallman)

Rusty was happy to give the new champion, Bill Elliott, a smile and a handshake in victory lane at Atlanta, but he admitted to reporters, "This thing is gnawing at me right now. There's always next year, but I hate to let this one slip away." (David Chobat)

Rusty came to the season finale at Atlanta still trailing Elliott for the championship. He had to go all out if he hoped to have any chance of overtaking him. And he did. Here Rusty battles under Dale Earnhardt on his way to a 4.25-second victory over Davey Allison. (Wallace collection)

Rusty won again in another wild finish at North Wilkesboro, this time with Geoff Bodine. Bodine hit Rusty in the rear in the first turn of the last lap and muscled past. But Rusty returned the favor in turn three, shoving Bodine out of the groove. Rusty won by a car length over Phil Parsons as Bodine finished third.

At Rockingham, Rusty cut a tire early in the race and fell to twenty-third. Again he fought back to the front. He won by 13.5 seconds over Ricky Rudd. "We've been down before, but we were able to bounce back," he said after the race. "I think we have the number-one team, and I'm driving like it's number one. If we lose the championship, it will be very disheartening. Even if we do lose, I will feel like we've won it."

Rusty had set a new personal record. He had won three Winston Cup races in a row. But it didn't make much of a dent in Elliott's points lead. While Rusty was winning, Elliott was finishing fourth, fifth, and fourth. With only two races remaining, Rusty was still seventy-nine points behind. And at Phoenix, while Alan Kulwicki was winning his first Winston Cup race, Rusty was losing even more ground. He finished fifth, but Elliott was fourth. Rusty led a lap; Elliott didn't. So they tied in points for the race. Rusty was still seventy-nine points behind.

So Elliott needed to finish only eighteenth or higher in the final race at Atlanta to win his first NASCAR Winston Cup championship. And that's all Elliott aimed to do. He raced conservatively, finished eleventh, and won his first title by twenty-four points. Rusty did all he could to catch up. He led 174 of the 328 laps and won by 4.25 seconds over Davey Allison. It was his fourth victory in five races. He had finished in the top ten in every race but two since Talladega in May. He had posted sixteen top-five finishes in those twenty races, including six victories. But it was not enough.

"I did what I had to do," Rusty said at the time. "I couldn't believe the way he was running. I thought he would come here and race for it."

Said Elliott: "Rusty did what he had to do, and I did what I had to do."

The celebration in victory lane at North Carolina Motor Speedway in Rockingham was particularly intense after Rusty's victory in the AC Delco 500. He lost three laps early when he cut a tire and had to make an unscheduled pit stop, but he made up the laps and won by 13.5 seconds over Ricky Rudd. Team owner Raymond Beadle (next to Rusty), and crewman John Dodson (far right) share in the festivities.

"We dug a little deeper and told ourselves that we were not going to be denied in 1989. When faced with any kind of adversity, we drew together."

As the 1989 Winston Cup season got under way, the momentum had been building for Rusty and the Blue Max team for three years. He had won in his fifth race with the team and improved year by year.

Rusty gathered the team together. Besides Dodson and Harold Elliott, there was Jimmy Makar, Todd Parrott, Buddy "Red Dog" Barnes, David Evans, Harold Koshimizu, and Dodson's young brothers, John and Brad. They talked among themselves and made a mutual commitment: 1989 would be their year. No matter what they had to do, no matter how hard they had to work, no matter what obstacles faced them, they would find a way to win the championship in 1989. They had fought back throughout 1988 and had come to recognize that one of their strongest attributes was the ability to thrive on adversity.

"In 1989, we made the decision to win," Rusty says. "I heard a woman tennis player use that term on television, and it hit me right in the head: So we made the decision to win. The 'decision to win' is a whole lot different than saying, 'Oh, we'll do better this year.' The decision to win was expecting more out of your crew than they thought they were going to be putting out. And it was expecting the wives and girlfriends to give up what they didn't want to give up—time with their husbands or boyfriends. It was the team expected to be together more. It was the decision to work around the clock in the middle of the week to rebuild your pole-winning motor, and then taking it to the next track and sitting on the pole again. And this extra effort really paid off."

"I think losing by just a scant few points in 1988 is what really told us we could do it," says Dodson. "We dug a little deeper and told ourselves that we were not going to be denied in 1989. When faced with any kind of adversity, we drew together."

Rusty found himself in victory lane for the third time in six starts after The Valleydale Meats 500. The race featured an astounding 20 caution flags, most caused by crashes that sent eight cars to the garage early. Rusty beat out Darrell Waltrip over the last 15 laps to win. (David Chobat)

The fans were on their feet and roaring as Rusty took the checkered flag to win the GM Goodwrench 500 at North Carolina Motor Speedway on March 5, 1989. Rusty came back from two laps down to beat Alan Kulwicki by 1.6 seconds. (David Chobat)

But even before the first race, as the team prepared for Daytona, trouble was brewing. Raymond Beadle's financial problems had spread to his stock car team. Rusty was supposed to be paid $85,816 by December 31 to cover all outstanding 1988 salary and prize money. The check didn't come. Rusty agreed to one extension, then another. A different payment of $25,000 to cover the first portion of Rusty's $300,000 salary in 1989 was due January 15. It didn't arrive either.

"All this sponsor money was coming in, and Raymond started to use some of it for other purposes besides the race team," Miller says. "At first there were just little delays. But by the end of 1988, it was scary enough that we had to try to make sure it didn't get any further out of hand. We had to put him on notice."

On January 19, Miller wrote a letter to Beadle. He demanded immediate payment of all the money owed Rusty. And he notified Beadle that as far as Rusty was concerned, their contract had been voided. But it was more a threat than a promise. Rusty didn't have anywhere else to go.

It was difficult to press the issue with the fun-loving, ever optimistic Beadle. "When you were with Raymond, you couldn't help but like the guy," Miller says. "He'd say,

Although Waltrip was angry after Rusty spun him out during their duel for victory on the last lap of the Winston, they were on good terms again within a few weeks. This photograph of the two seasoned NASCAR drivers was taken later in the season. (David Chobat)

Rusty gets air as he bounces off the curb on the inside of turn two at Sears Point International Raceway. Rusty and Ricky Rudd had a spirited, fender-banging duel on the last lap before Rudd prevailed. Rusty was second. (David Chobat)

Rusty charges through turn three at Watkins Glen International on his way to his fourth victory of the 1989 season. Rusty took the lead with fourteen laps to go and won by 1.01 seconds over Mark Martin. (David Chobat)

Opposite: Rusty waves to the crowd as he pops out of his Pontiac in victory lane at Watkins Glen. The victory on the 2.428-mile circuit was his fourth road course win in six races. (David Chobat)

'Don't worry about that. We'll get it squared away, no problem.' He was real loose. He had his priorities, and he'd take care of his priorities in due fashion."

"He wouldn't let me get in too much trouble," Rusty says. "He'd try to take care of me. He'd give me some money and say, 'I'm a little short—I'll get you next week.' But Raymond did so much for my career, even with all the problems we had, I can sit back right now and can't ever get mad at him."

Rusty burst out of the blocks in 1989 with three victories in the first six races, winning at Rockingham, Richmond, and Bristol. At Rockingham, he came back from two laps down and eventually won by 1.6 seconds. At Richmond, Alan Kulwicki was running away with the race until a late caution period allowed Rusty to close the gap and pass Kulwicki for the lead. At Bristol, he avoided all the trouble that led to twenty yellow flags—a record—to win by a couple of car lengths over Darrell Waltrip.

"Things were really rolling at that point," Miller says. "Rusty had reached a level of driving ability that matched his car. And that car and him were like one. He could do things on the racetrack with that car that nobody else could do. He could have it sideways with one tire in the dirt and still make the pass. From the outside, it looked like a huge, wonderful lifestyle. Everybody was happy—rocking and rolling. But within the organization there was trouble."

"Raymond just couldn't fund it," Rusty says. "Things really didn't start to unravel until the championship year. But it didn't matter to me. I had blinders on to it. I wasn't worried about it because we were running so damn good. I wasn't going to let anything distract us. Raymond was like a cat. The sucker had nine lives. Every time he'd get down, he'd find a way to get back up. So I never worried about it. But I was winning, and the checks weren't showing up. So we had to get serious about it. I didn't know it at the time, but the guy who pretty well funded us in 1989 was Rick Hendrick. Rick was helping Raymond, and he ended up taking over the assets. I had a two-owner team and I didn't know it."

As the series headed to Charlotte for the Winston and the Coca-Cola 600, rumors were percolating about the problems with the team and Rusty's status. Rusty called a press conference.

"He could do things on the racetrack with that car that nobody else could do. He could have it sideways with one tire in the dirt and still make the pass."

"I've been hearing and reading all this stuff about me leaving to go here and there and do all kinds of crazy things," he told reporters. "We don't need people hounding us. Pressure is great, but unnecessary pressure and untrue tales aren't. I'm happy with this team. We have a good team, and we're going to stay together."

Rusty admitted there were problems. And he said he did not expect to drive for Beadle in 1990. "But Raymond has said he is going to straighten out the problems, and I am confident he will," he said.

After his testy press conference, Rusty carried his take-no-prisoners attitude to the track. With two laps remaining in the Winston, Rusty was chasing Darrell Waltrip through turn three. Waltrip's car drifted up the banking a bit as Rusty closed the gap. Rusty never let up. The two cars touched. Waltrip spun. Rusty won.

"I never got out of the gas," Rusty says. "I was going for it. I got my nose right up to him and we touched and he went around. He didn't do anything wrong. It was my fault. But it was for $200,000, and I was real aggressive."

Waltrip, so often the villain, was now the victim. "I hope he chokes on that $200,000," an angry Waltrip declared on national television. Rusty, who wanted only to be liked by the fans, now found himself instantly vilified. A few fans tossed beer cans on the track

Rusty's Blue Max crew changes the left-side tires during a pit stop on Rusty's way to victory in the 1989 Miller 400 on September 10 at Richmond International Raceway. The win was Rusty's sixth and last victory of his Winston Cup championship season. (David Chobat)

during the last lap. The rival crews scuffled as Rusty's team pushed his car toward victory lane. Rusty was horrified by the intense fan reaction. Charlotte Motor Speedway President H. A. "Humpy" Wheeler sent two armed guards home with Rusty.

To Rusty, losing his fans wasn't worth winning the race. He couldn't tolerate it. He and Waltrip were on speaking terms again in two or three races. But it took a year before all the fans were over it. "That was one of the scariest things I've ever gone through," he says.

A week after the Winston, Rusty led the Coca-Cola 600 twice before his engine blew. He finished thirty-first and plummeted to seventh in points. Through June and July, Rusty bounced back and forth between near perfection and poor results. He finished second to Ricky Rudd after another wild last lap at California's Sears Point Raceway. But at Pocono, after winning the pole and leading five times, he ruptured an oil cooler and finished twenty-second. He finished second at Michigan, then seventeenth at Daytona. He was second in the second Pocono race, then crashed at Talladega and finished thirty-seventh. Heading into Watkins Glen, where he had won three of the previous five races, Rusty was fifth in points.

The financial problems at Blue Max Racing were causing new headaches, especially for Dodson and Harold Elliott. "We went to some racetracks where we weren't supposed to get any tires because we hadn't paid the tire bills," Dodson says. "Our truck was held at the scales in Barstow, California, because we weren't insured properly. So here we are, contending for the championship, and we're trying to get across country on a shoestring. I'm at the hotel on the phone trying to make sure our race car gets in town on time.

"My biggest job was plugging the holes in the ship," Dodson continues. "It was hard. But the approach we took was, 'If we don't win, we might not be here next week.' One thing about it. Raymond never tried to run the race team. I think that was a key to our success. When the problems came up, I'd call Raymond, and he could always take care of them. He could pull a rabbit out of a hat. I'd tell him, 'Here's our next mountain. How are you going to climb it?'

"Raymond Beadle would give you the shirt off his back if he could. He invested a lot of money in the team. You gotta love Raymond to death. But we didn't really know what was going on. We just knew things weren't getting paid on time, including us."

It didn't stop the Blue Max team from enjoying themselves. "We were a bunch of renegades," says Dodson, who today is a consultant for the Number 35 Team Amick Chevrolet and driver Lyndon Amick. "We played hard and we raced hard. A lot of teams envied us. And after 1988, we would not be denied again. Besides, it was our last chance. We knew it."

An exhausted, dehydrated Rusty flashes across the finish line on the 400th lap at Richmond. The race-day temperature was in the mid-90s, but Rusty opted against wearing a cool suit. "It was the dumbest thing I've ever done," he said after the race. "I started losing my concentration in the last fifty laps." (David Chobat)

On lap 428 at Rockingham, Rusty collides with Dale Earnhardt and sends him into a spin. Rusty's second-place finish put him 109 points ahead of Earnhardt in the championship race. Mark Martin won the event for his first career Winston Cup victory. (Jeff Robinson)

"Probably the biggest thing I remember about the season was how much fun we had," said Jimmy Makar, a crewman on the team. Makar is now the crew chief for Bobby Labonte and the Joe Gibbs–owned Number 18 Pontiac. "But we were always on a shoe-string. That was our MO. Eventually, we always got a paycheck. It might be two or three weeks late, or it might bounce, but Raymond always made good on it. I was real fortunate because the bank kinda knew what was going on after it happened a time or two. And I had a friend who would call me and tell me it happened again so I didn't get caught by it."

"We had finally got the 1988 debts settled in February 1989," Miller says. "Then he missed the next payment in 1989. It just got worse and worse. Raymond became very hard to get a hold of. I had to send him registered letters. Amazing stuff was going on. The guys would get their paychecks and run to the bank, and only about half of them would get cashed. Finally, after about five months of this, we got an attorney."

On July 25, two days after the Pocono race, in the midst of a Winston Cup championship points battle, Rusty filed suit in Mecklenburg County Superior Court in Charlotte against his car owner. He demanded that Beadle pay all the money owed him. And he asked to be released from his contract for the 1990 season.

Then Rusty went out and won back-to-back races at Watkins Glen and Michigan for his fourth and fifth victories of the season. He pummeled the field at Michigan, beating runner-up Morgan Shepherd by more than 15 seconds. And he told reporters afterward, "Even though Raymond and I are having trouble off the track, it will not interfere with our efforts to win the championship." He was now second in points, eighty-two behind leader Dale Earnhardt.

Two days after the Bristol race, where Rusty finished sixth, Beadle filed a counter suit. Beadle claimed that Rusty was trying to break a valid contract.

The next weekend, in the Southern 500, Rusty finished fourth but was still seventy-three points behind Earnhardt, who won the race. At Richmond, in mid-90-degree heat, Rusty was barely able to finish. He was exhausted, and he ran out of gas on the last lap, but he coasted across the finish line 7.41 seconds ahead of Earnhardt for his sixth victory of the year.

In the final race at Atlanta, it was all Rusty could do to hang on. Here he takes the upper groove while Alan Kulwicki runs in the center of the turn and an ultraquick Dale Earnhardt, who ran away with the race, blows past in the bottom groove. (Brian Cleary)

With five races to go, Rusty was still seventy-five points behind Earnhardt. But the break he needed came at Charlotte. Earnhardt broke a camshaft on lap 14 and finished last. Rusty was eighth. Suddenly he was leading the points again, thirty-five ahead of Earnhardt. "It's about time Dale had some bad luck," he said. "I know how it feels."

Now the series moved to North Wilkesboro, where it all came down to the final lap. Ricky Rudd, no friend of Earnhardt's, got under him going into the first turn on the last lap. They collided. Both drivers spun. Earnhardt lost the lead, finished tenth, and unleashed a profanity-studded tirade about Rudd on national television. Rusty finished a quiet seventh and gained two points.

At Rockingham on October 22, as Mark Martin won his first Winston Cup race, Earnhardt was already two laps down when Rusty accidentally collided with him in turn three, dropping him further back. Earnhardt finished twentieth. Wallace finished second. With two races to go, Rusty led by 109 points.

Five days later, Rusty and Beadle settled their legal battle. Rusty agreed to race for Beadle in 1990. "Through all of this, Rusty never bobbled," Don Miller says. "He would say, 'As long as the guys don't get down, we'll be OK. You take care of this, Don, and I'll run the car.' But he never changed. It was as if he was on a railroad track, crossing the next bridge just before it fell. But he never wavered. He was absolutely the pillar of that whole operation. And once Raymond countersued, we came to realize that the best resolution to the whole thing was to settle. After we went to court for the first time, we could see that the only guys who were going to win were the attorneys."

Rusty arrived in Phoenix with renewed resolve to clinch the championship. And he was well on his way to doing that, leading with less than 70 miles to go, when he passed a car driven by Hollywood stuntman Stan Barrett going into turn one. Barrett lost his brakes, ran into the back of Rusty, and sent him into the first turn wall.

Rusty's sixteenth-place finish opened the door for Martin and Earnhardt. He led Martin by seventy-eight points, Earnhardt by seventy-nine. He needed to finish nineteenth or better at the final race at Atlanta to win the championship. And Rusty discovered what many title contenders know, that the final test for the Winston Cup was the most difficult of all. Nothing went right at Atlanta. After a year of running with the leaders, week in and week out, Rusty suddenly found the challenge of securing nineteenth place almost overwhelming. He started fourth but quickly dropped back. He pitted early, was caught by a yellow flag, and lost a lap.

"It was excruciating," Dodson recalls. "Some of the things that happened didn't make any sense. One time Rusty thought he had a flat tire and pitted. He didn't. Another time, he had made a full 90-mile green stop run and he came in for right side tires. He took off, and three laps later, Rusty came on the radio and said the left rear wheel was loose. Well, we had not changed the lefts. They already had 100 miles on them before the wheel came loose."

When Rusty pitted, the left rear wheel *was* loose. Dodson had never seen anything like it, before or since. The only thing he could figure was the tire was "borderline loose" during much of the previous run, and the jarring stop and start of the pit stop loosened it enough to create a vibration.

"At the time, it was like somebody, some force, was trying to keep us from winning," Dodson says. "My little brother, John, came up to me. He changed the left rear tire. He was crying. He said, 'I just cost us the championship.' I told him, 'No, you didn't. Remember, we're all in this together.' You could feel it slipping away. I had to coach myself not to show it, because everybody was looking at me. But I enjoyed that day. We were up to it—not intimidated by it. As far as we were concerned, it was just another day when we had to find a way to claw back."

Rusty fell back as far as thirty-third, four laps down. "I had to tell him we were in positions that we weren't a time or two," Dodson says. But Rusty crept back up in the standings—twenty-fifth, nineteenth, seventeenth, and finally fifteenth. And that is where he finished. Dale Earnhardt ran away with the race. When the points were totaled, Rusty had won the championship by twelve points.

"As sloppy as it looked," Rusty said afterward, "this is still the highlight of my career."

After passing his survival test at Atlanta, Rusty holds the season-long Winston Cup championship trophy he had spent all of his adult life chasing. His twelve-point victory over Dale Earnhardt gave him a $1 million bonus from the R. J. Reynolds Tobacco Company. (David Chobat)

"They come through the tri-oval! Checkered is waving! Ernie Irvan wins! And Rusty spins and gets airborne! And flips wildly right at the finish line!"

Sitting on the roof of a Winston Cup promotional car, Rusty felt as if he owned New York during the weekend of his championship banquet in December. As the champ, he worked tirelessly making personal appearances on behalf of the sport. (David Chobat)

Opposite: Rusty's car was nearly vertical when he cartwheeled across the finish line in sixth place in the 1993 Winston 500 at Talladega. He had moved down to block Dale Earnhardt and the two collided. That hit turned Rusty's car around and it became airborne, ending in this terrifying crash. (Jeff Robinson)

For Rusty, the culmination of more than twenty years of work—and one long season of triumph and turmoil—came at the NASCAR Winston Cup awards banquet in New York City in December 1989.

It was time for celebration, but Rusty vowed: "I'm going to be the best champion I can be." He threw himself into a dizzying schedule of public appearances, despite an unpleasant incident four days before the final race at Atlanta.

At the end of a 2-hour charity autograph session, Rusty was approached by a man who congratulated him on his season, then said, "Come Sunday, I hope you drop dead." The shock caused Rusty to question whether winning the championship was worth it. In typical fashion, he got over it quickly and eagerly tackled all the extra duties of a champion.

Rusty's legal settlement with Beadle put him back in the driver's seat of Beadle's Number 27 Pontiac for one more season. But the team's sponsor, Kodiak, was leaving. Roger Penske and Don Miller came to the rescue. They learned of Miller Brewing Company's interest in sponsoring a car, so they helped broker a long-term contract between the beer company and Rusty and brought sponsorship to Beadle for Rusty's final year.

"We had relationships with Miller Brewing prior to them coming with the team," Penske says. "So I was the glue between Rusty, Don and the team, and Miller. And it's been a good relationship. There's no individual out there in the racing business that works as hard for the sponsors as Rusty. He's still willing to go out after a bad weekend and do whatever you have to do to keep the sponsors happy."

"Roger was sending me a lot of letters," Rusty says. "Every time I'd win a race, he would send me a congratulatory letter. He'd say he was keeping his eye on me."

When Hut Stricklin clipped fenders with Rusty coming out of turn four shortly after the halfway point of the Winston 500 at Talladega, Rusty spun, and Dale Jarrett, driving the Wood Brothers Ford, slammed the outside wall. Jarrett and two others were eliminated. Rusty hobbled to a twentieth-place finish. (Brian Cleary)

Rusty talks with crewman Jimmy Makar in May 1990 at Charlotte Motor Speedway. Makar took over as crew chief in 1991 after Barry Dodson left to join a new team. (Elmer Kappell)

Rusty's first victory in 1990 was the Coca-Cola 600, which he thoroughly dominated. And when he won at Sears Point—his fifth road course victory in seven races—he moved into third place in the championship. "Now we've just got to stay out of trouble," Rusty said. "One little problem and you can lose a ton of points."

But Rusty had more than one little problem as the season progressed. The Sears Point victory was his last of 1990, and while he posted five more top-five finishes, he also failed to finish six races. He suffered engine failures in races at Talladega and Watkins Glen, lost another engine in the Southern 500, and then blew three in a row at Charlotte, Rockingham, and Phoenix.

Rusty slumped to sixth in the 1990 points chase as Earnhardt held off Martin for the championship. The magic was gone at Blue Max Racing. Dodson had left in early September to accept a lucrative offer—$200,000 in 1991 to run Team III, a new Winston Cup team.

"After Miller Brewing came on board, it really didn't seem that much better on the financial side of it, at least in the shop," Dodson says. "So you started to wonder, 'Is it going to get any better?' It just seemed like the trend was never going to end. On top of that, people were coming at us from every angle, trying to dismantle what we had put together."

If this is the condition of Rusty's car, then the track must be Daytona or Talladega. Here Rusty goes back out on the track with the remains of his Pontiac after becoming involved in a fourteen-car crash on lap 92 of the 1992 Daytona 500. He completed 150 of the 200 laps and finished thirty-first. (Elmer Kappell)

Above: Dale Earnhardt, four laps down, gives leader Rusty Wallace a push during a caution period for rain in the Miller Genuine Draft 500 at Pocono International Raceway on July 21, 1991. Rusty was wondering whether he might run out of fuel during the yellow flag laps when Earnhardt radioed the message: "Let me push you around a couple of laps." Rusty won when rain ended the race a couple of laps later. (Larry McTighe)

Right: Rusty works on his restrictor plate engine with his crew in the garage at Talladega Superspeedway in 1992. He finished eleventh in both Talladega races in 1992. (Nigel Kinrade)

"Thirty-four races [without a win] was starting to wear real, real thin. I was really getting nervous. I knew I had everything in the world to do it with. I had the car, the motors. We just couldn't get all the talent we had organized."

The end was obviously coming. In July 1989, when the suit was filed, Rusty had confirmed to reporters that he and Don Miller had begun talks with Penske and Miller Brewing. By October 1990, Rusty and Miller were busy organizing their new team. They had Miller Brewing as their sponsor, of course, and announced on October 29 that they were building their shop, to be finished by December, in Lakeside Business Park, a new industrial park next to Interstate 77 in Mooresville, North Carolina.

After working twenty years with friend and mentor Roger Penske, Miller was moving to North Carolina to become the general manager of Rusty's new team.

"You really are serious about this," Penske said.

"Yes," replied Miller.

"Then let's do it together."

So as the 1991 season was about to start, Rusty announced that he had become partners with Miller and Penske to form Penske Racing South. Penske owned 52 percent and Miller and Rusty had 24 percent apiece. Jimmy Makar was the new crew chief, and Harold Elliott had joined as head engine builder.

At Daytona, Penske explained why he returned to NASCAR. "We're using this as a business venture," he said. "One of our strongest markets is the Southeast for our truck leasing business. We probably have 15,000 trucks running in the NASCAR market area. I love to see the truckers come in the plant in Detroit and say, 'We can't wait to see you run on the NASCAR circuit.' And we use it as a customer entertainment medium. Racing has been a common thread throughout our businesses for years. What I've been most impressed with is the two guys themselves [Rusty and Miller] have spent 20 hours a day at the shop pulling the thing together."

Six events into the season, at Bristol, Rusty won his first race under the banner of Penske South. "We're building a new team, and we're back," he said. But he won only one more race—at Pocono in July. The season was spoiled by inconsistency. He failed to finish ten of the twenty-nine races and ended up tenth in points. The highlight of the season was Rusty's success in the IROC series. He won three straight races and the championship.

But the Winston Cup team was still sorting itself out. Two days after the Pocono victory, Makar announced that he was leaving to join his brother-in-law, Dale Jarrett, with the new team being formed by Washington Redskins coach Joe Gibbs.

The year 1992 got off to an awful start. Rusty didn't even finish in the top ten until the sixth race, at Bristol, where he was ninth. When the series reached Watkins Glen in August, he had recorded only five top-tens and only two top-fives. Rusty finished sixth at the Glen. That weekend, veteran crew chief Buddy Parrott joined the team.

Parrott had been with Darrell Waltrip when he was blossoming in the late '70s. He had guided Richard Petty to his 200th victory and helped Derrike Cope win the 1990

The crew did their best to get Rusty out of the pits quickly during the Pepsi 400. At the beginning of the season, crew chief Buddy Parrott boldly predicted that Rusty would win ten races. Now July, Rusty had yet to win a single race and on this day finished ninth. (Nigel Kinrade)

For seven laps, Rusty and Darrell Waltrip ran door to door as they battled for the lead in the Miller Genuine Draft 400 at Richmond International Raceway on September 12, 1992. Rusty finally took the lead on lap 240 and won going away, beating Mark Martin by 3.59 seconds. (Larry McTighe)

Daytona 500. Parrott had passion and a burning desire to win. It didn't take long for his enthusiasm to rub off on the team. One month later, at Richmond, Rusty scored his first victory in more than a year.

"Thirty-four races [without a win] was starting to wear real, real thin," Rusty said afterward. "I was really getting nervous. I knew I had everything in the world to do it with. I had the car, the motors. We had a bunch of good people at the shop. We just couldn't get all the talent we had organized. Now that Buddy is over here, we have someone to look up to with some maturity."

Richmond was Rusty's only victory in 1992. He was thirteenth in points, his worst finish since 1985. But heading into the 1993 season, momentum was building again. Parrott was building it.

"I'd never had anything like that to work with," says Parrott, who manages two of Jack Roush's teams today. "It was just unbelievable. The resources. The beautiful shop. And I saw that all we needed to do was just stir the people up a little bit."

In January 1993, the motorsports media visited Rusty's shop during Charlotte Motor Speedway's annual media tour. "I sat up there in front of everybody and said, 'This team is good enough to win ten races,'" Parrott remembers. "And Rusty looked over at me like, 'What are you talking about?'" Rusty, nevertheless, loved the brashness of it.

But danger, as well as tragedy, loomed in 1993. Rusty was having a great Daytona 500 until lap 169, when Derrike Cope and Michael Waltrip collided coming off turn two. Rusty saw it coming. He tried to avoid them to the inside. He didn't make it. His car was turned sideways. It lifted off the ground. And then it launched into one of the most spectacular crashes ever at Daytona.

Rusty barrel-rolled twice, flipped end over end one-and-a-half times, and then barrel-rolled four or five more times. "I was saying, 'Man, this is great. I'm finally going to get a good Daytona 500 in.' And then it happened," Rusty says. "I was alert the whole time. I can't remember if I closed my eyes or not. But I was with it the whole time. I knew what was going on. It happened so fast. *Bam! Bam! Bam! Bam! Bam! Splat!* And then I'm OK.

"Every time I hit, I was just saying, 'I hope this isn't a bad one here.' It would hit and then it would go in the air. And when it would get ready to land, you'd just say to yourself, 'Oh man, I hope this isn't going to be one of these death-defying, uncontrollable ones that knocks you out.' And it never came."

Rusty crawled out with only two cuts under his chin that took six stitches to close. He was more angry than anything else. Back in the garage, he told reporters, "It was upsetting, but it's over, and everything is cool." The most costly part of the accident turned out to be the loss in points because he finished thirty-second.

But he shook off Daytona by going on a tear. He won at Rockingham and announced: "I've never been so dedicated to anything as I am to winning the Winston Cup championship this year. My team is in good shape, and we're ready to be champions."

He finished second to Davey Allison in Richmond. He was third in the Atlanta race, which had been snowed out and postponed a week by the great blizzard of '93. At Darlington, Rusty finished fifth, one position ahead of Winston Cup champion Alan Kulwicki. The next stop was Bristol.

Kulwicki never made it. On the evening of Thursday, April 1, the plane carrying him to Bristol fell out of the sky while approaching the airport. Kulwicki and three others were killed instantly.

"It was devastating," Rusty recalls. "I was at the hotel, and people started coming in and saying, 'There's been a crash out there.' Barry Dodson came in and said that. Alan and I had raced against each other all the way back to the USAC days. I helped him get his first major Winston Cup sponsor. I was the one who told him to hire Paul Andrews. So I got in a car and drove out to the airport, and sure enough, it had happened. We all wondered why. He had been coming in right behind Earnhardt's plane. Then the report finally came out later that said it was a simultaneous dual flameout because of ice ingestion."

Wallace ran away with the race nobody really wanted to run, then saluted the fallen champion with a backward "Polish" victory lap, which Kulwicki had performed after his first victory in Phoenix in 1988. The next weekend, at North Wilkesboro, Rusty won again—his third victory in seven races. It gave him the lead in the Winston Cup points championship. "Winning

This crash at Daytona was the first of two big crashes in Rusty's spectacular 1993 campaign. It did not hurt him physically, but it killed him in points. He had run with the leaders during the race, but the crash dropped him to a thirty-second-place finish and cost him more than the eighty points that separated him from Winston Cup champion Dale Earnhardt at the end of the season. (Daytona News-Journal)

these many races this quick has exceeded my expectations," he said after the race. "I thought we'd win three or four races this year, but I didn't know they would come in the first seven races of the year. The way our team is right now, I sure don't put ten wins out of the question."

At Martinsville, he made it four for eight with another dominating performance, leading 409 of 500 laps.

"I guess we're all racing for second now," said Dale Jarrett.

"There's nothing trick here," Wallace said. "We have a motor that's strong, that's not blowing up. We've got a maintenance program that's second to none. We've got a better pit crew and a better car. I never thought I'd win every race in a month. It's a pretty wild deal. I've got this feeling in my blood right now like I had at the end of 1988. . . . I'm going down to Talladega next week just thinking about keeping it out of the wrecks."

At Talladega, as at Daytona, Rusty was strong. He started twenty-fourth but sliced through the pack to take the lead on lap 19. He stayed there for seventeen laps. He also led twenty-one laps late in the race until a brief shower caused a yellow flag and a final two-lap shoot-out among the fifteen lead-lap cars. It was one of the wildest finishes in NASCAR history. Some drivers didn't know where they finished. Some criticized NASCAR for allowing such a potentially dangerous sprint.

Rusty bounced back from the Daytona crash and won the first of his ten victories of the 1993 season in the Goodwrench 400 at Rockingham. Here his pit crew services his car as Winston Cup champion Alan Kulwicki drives past on pit road. One month after this race, Kulwicki perished in a plane crash at Bristol. (Nigel Kinrade)

"I was in and out, in and out, in and out after the crash," he recalls. "Physically, it was a real blow. I was black and blue everywhere."

In the race to the line, Rusty pulled down to block Dale Earnhardt. ESPN anchor Bob Jenkins called the finish: "They come through the tri-oval! Checkered is waving! Ernie Irvan wins! And Rusty spins and gets airborne! And flips wildly right at the start/finish line!"

Jenkins's voice dropped instantly, subdued by the vicious horror of the crash. "Very reminiscent of his accident at Daytona," he said quietly.

But it was worse. At Daytona, Rusty had avoided hard hits. His car had moved almost like a rock skipping across water. At Talladega, his car slammed to earth again and again, hitting hard on nearly all of its nine flips.

The last thing Rusty remembered was seeing his wrist bend grotesquely and break away from the steering wheel as the car hit hard. He was cut from the wreckage and airlifted to Carraway Methodist Medical Center in Birmingham.

"I was in and out, in and out, in and out after the crash," he recalls. "I remember I was out in the helicopter for a while. And I was in and out at the hospital for a while. Physically, it was a real blow. I was black and blue everywhere. My face was bruised. My wrist was broke."

He spent two nights in the Birmingham hospital, then was flown to Indianapolis, where noted motorsports orthopedic surgeon Terry Trammell inserted a pin lengthwise in his wrist. Rusty, in typical fashion, quickly recovered his spirits. Four days after the crash, he did an hour-long teleconference. "I pulled down to make a block on [Earnhardt]," Rusty said. "But he was going a lot faster than me. He thought he could have got off the gas quicker. But I felt if I wouldn't have pulled in front of him that abruptly, it wouldn't have happened. It's a rough deal, but there's no hard feelings. We're real good friends. He showed a lot of concern. He called three or four times. He was just a real gentleman about the whole deal."

Rusty finished sixth at Talladega, even though his car was vertical when it crossed the finish line. But the crash broke his momentum and helped send his season into a tailspin from which he was never able to recover.

"We went to Sears Point, and I broke second gear in the race," he says. "That really hurt. In the 600 at Charlotte, I got the car loose coming off turn two and I couldn't back steer because my wrist brace was locking up on me. I could only turn the wheel so far. I had to spin the car. I got into the wall. That really hurt." He had another hard crash at Dover. And he blew an engine and finished thirty-ninth at Pocono. He plummeted to fifth in points.

Opposite: This spectacular sequence shows Rusty's horrible crash after he flew across the finish line to finish sixth in the 1993 Winston 500 at Talladega. The crash did not hurt Rusty in points, but it left him bruised, beat up, and with a broken left wrist. He came back strong, however, and won six more races in 1993 after the crash. (Jeff Robinson)

With a special glove and bandage covering his broken left wrist, Rusty talks with Todd Parrott as the team prepares his car for the 1993 Winston. The injury hampered Rusty's ability to turn the steering wheel, and he spun and crashed in the Coca-Cola 600, which followed the all-star race. Rusty finished eighth in the Winston. (Nigel Kinrade)

When the series arrived in New Hampshire for the Slick 50 300 on July 11, Rusty had climbed back to third in points. He started thirty-third, and it took him more than half the race to get to the front. When a late yellow brought leader Davey Allison and the rest of the front-runners to the pits, Rusty's crew added more luster to its growing reputation as the fastest pit crew by sending him back out first.

"Hey Rusty, we're *baaaaaack,*" crew chief Buddy Parrott said in a singsong voice on the team radio after Rusty took the checkered flag for his fifth victory of the year, winning by 1.31 seconds over Mark Martin.

"You guys did a great job," Wallace radioed back. "They're all giving us a bunch of crap about being dead. We're not dead. We were just takin' a break."

The next afternoon, tragedy struck again. Davey Allison was fatally injured when his helicopter crashed as he landed in the infield at Talladega. For the second time in four months, a top NASCAR driver had perished not on the track, but in an aviation accident.

"The last time I saw Davey was at Loudon [New Hampshire]," Rusty says. "We had been racing. And after I won, he pulled up alongside me and gave me a big thumbs-up. We were supposed to go in my airplane to Milwaukee together later that week. I got a call at home from one of his crewmen, Joey Knuckles. He said, 'I think something has happened to Davey.' And all of a sudden my phone started ringing off the hook with calls from all these aviation people I know. That was another one that was really devastating."

Meanwhile, the effects of his Talladega crash continued to affect Rusty through the summer. At New Hampshire, even in victory, his wrist still "felt like a toothache." He dominated the entire race at Bristol on August 28, only to lose the lead to Mark Martin with thirteen laps to go because he was tired and his neck ached. "Everything from that darn Talladega wreck is hurting tonight," he said after finishing second.

Although he was unable to catch Dale Earnhardt for the Winston Cup championship, Rusty achieved another goal in the season-ending Hooters 500 at Atlanta. He won the race, giving him a career-high ten victories in one year and fulfilling Buddy Parrott's preseason prediction. (Nigel Kinrade)

But after Bristol, Rusty mounted another charge. He finished third in the Southern 500, then won two straight at Richmond and Dover. He was now second in points, 181 behind Earnhardt. And after Rusty won his eighth race of the season at North Wilkesboro, he pulled to within seventy-two points. Three weeks later, he won again at Rockingham, where his pit crew won the Unocal Pit Crew competition with a record speed. But Earnhardt's lead was still seventy-two points.

Earnhardt all but locked up the title at Phoenix. Rusty was running in fourth on lap 190 when a tire went flat in the fourth turn and pieces of flailing rubber battered his front end before he could reach the pits. He lost two laps during

the long pit stop to fix the damage and finished nineteenth. Earnhardt finished fourth and led by 126 points before the final race at Atlanta.

"When we lost that tire at Phoenix, that was one of the biggest things that cost us the championship," Parrott says. "We got caught up in winning races. We did things with tire pressures that maybe we shouldn't have. I think we were probably the first team to go out on a limb and go lower than Goodyear's recommended air pressure. So we made our own problem."

Earnhardt won the championship by eighty points, but Rusty did all he could to challenge. He dominated the final race at Atlanta and won by more than 5 seconds. He finished second in the championship, even after winning ten races and leading 28 percent of all the laps run. After the race, Rusty and Earnhardt circled the track side by side with a Polish victory lap and a final salute to Kulwicki and Allison.

Says Parrott, "Afterwards, Rusty popped right out of his car like he normally does. And he looked at me and said, 'Didn't win the damn championship, but I got your ten races.' I'll always remember that."

"The crashes definitely killed the championship that year," Rusty says today. "I would have never thought I'd win ten races and not win the championship. Daytona really hurt in points, and Talladega really hurt me physically. It was a tough damn deal to handle. I just had to keep charging back. And I thought we charged back really, really good. But we just ran out of time."

The 1993 season marked the debut of Jeff Gordon, who became rookie of the year. Here Rusty chats with Gordon at Martinsville Speedway in a photograph taken in 1994. (Nigel Kinrade)

"I've been upside down at Daytona and I've been upside down at Talladega, and I'm telling you, it hurts."

En route to victory in the 1994 Hanes 500, Rusty leads Ernie Irvan down the frontstretch at Martinsville Speedway. Wallace's 16.1-second pit stop with sixty-eight laps to go allowed him to beat Irvan out of the pits and take the lead. He beat Irvan by about three car lengths. (Nigel Kinrade)

Opposite: Rusty and his son, Stephen, pose before the Winston at Charlotte Motor Speedway in 1998. Both Wallaces were racing that day, with Stephen competing in a Bandolero car earlier in the day and Rusty, of course, in the NASCAR all-star race that evening. (George Tiedemann)

As the Winston Cup series made its way back to Daytona International Speedway for the beginning of the 1994 season, everyone hoped for a quiet Speedweeks. The 1993 season had brought too much tragedy. But it was not to be.

Twenty-two minutes into the first practice, Neil Bonnett lost control of his car, hit the wall in turn four, and was fatally injured. Three days later, on a quiet, unhurried Monday morning, Rodney Orr died in a hideous crash coming off turn two. Never in NASCAR's long history had two drivers died in such a short span of time.

Patti had watched the Talladega crash in North Carolina on her living room television with their three children at her side. It had been a horrible moment. Now, at Daytona again, where she had seen Rusty flip twice, she was terrified. Rusty himself was worried by what he was seeing on the track.

"I saw some real wild and crazy driving going on in practice," he says. "A lot of drivers were under a lot of pressure to get the job done—drivers who didn't own their own teams but had rides they were just trying to keep. Neil died and Rodney Orr got killed. And what I didn't see was anybody giving a damn. Oh, everybody gave a damn. But it sure wasn't showing up in practice. I didn't feel a humble glow across the garage.

So I stood up in the driver's meeting."

Rusty spoke 2 hours before the start of the Twin 125s. "These cars just don't flip by themselves or spin out by themselves," he said. "I've been upside down at Daytona and I've been upside down at Talladega, and I'm telling you, it hurts. If Richard Childress loses Dale Earnhardt, he's out of business. If Felix Sabates loses Kyle Petty, he's out of business. I think everybody in this room is running scared. I'll tell you, my wife is damn scared. So use your heads, *please.*"

Rusty's victory in the Goody's 500 at Bristol International Raceway on the night of August 27, 1994, was his sixth of the season. He won eight for the year. Here he poses in victory lane with (left to right) crew chief Buddy Parrott, Penske Corporation executive Walt Czarnecki, Don Miller, and Roger Penske. (David Chobat)

In 1994 at Martinsville Speedway, Rusty talks with Don Miller, his friend and adviser for more than twenty years. Miller left his job with Roger Penske to become part-owner and general manager of Rusty's team in 1991, but in effect he stayed with Penske when Roger bought a majority share and created Penske Racing South. (Nigel Kinrade)

But in the 500, it was the same old story. On lap 63, Robert Pressley was bumped into the outside wall in turn four. Rusty became involved. "I picked a hole and was going for it, but Hut [Stricklin] couldn't get slowed down and got into the rear of me," Rusty said after yet another Daytona crash left him in forty-first place. "It was just one of those deals. Two weeks of all this stuff always ends up for me this way, at least the last four races down here."

But Rusty was back in victory lane seven days later, leading 346 out of 492 laps in his new Ford Thunderbird and winning by more than 5 seconds. It was his third victory in a row at the Rock, and it obviously didn't matter whether he was in a Pontiac or a Ford.

"We could probably win in a Jaguar out here," Rusty said afterward. The switch to Ford came after Rusty, Don Miller, and Roger Penske failed to negotiate a satisfactory new contract with Pontiac. General Motors was now running both its Chevy teams and its Pontiac teams under one entity known as the Motorsports Technology Group. Rusty believed the Pontiacs were getting shorted in the process. He switched to Ford, which was thrilled to get him.

The Rockingham race was just the first indication that the switch did not hurt his performance. Rusty won eight races in 1994. He was a terror on the short tracks, winning three of the eight races (both Martinsville races and the fall Bristol event) while posting four other top fives and finishing no worse than seventh in any of them. He won three in a row in June—at Dover, Pocono, and Michigan. And he won again at Dover in September.

Of all the victories in 1994, the most memorable was at Michigan. "I was leading the race all day long," he recalls. "It was a hot day, and the racetrack was coming apart. Everything was terrible—guys were crashing right and left. And we run out of gas."

Rusty had planned to pit on lap 175 of 200. But a yellow flag flew on that lap, and he had to make an extra lap while waiting for the pits to open. He ran out of gas and coasted down pit road. After many long, dramatic seconds, Parrott finally helped get the engine restarted by forcing ether into the carburetor. Rusty's Ford shot forward. Parrott tumbled to the ground. But they were back in the race.

"I was in eleventh position, but the problem I had was there were fourteen cars inside of me and ten cars in front of me," Rusty said. "It was just a hornet's nest. We just had to go quick. I took a couple of chancy moves and knocked off four cars

In this 1994 photograph, Rusty talks with Jeff Thousand (right) and other members of his team in the fabrication shop of Penske Racing South, located in Mooresville, North Carolina. (Nigel Kinrade)

Rusty leads Jeff Gordon up the hill and through turn two during the 1995 Save Mart 300. It was not one of his better road races. He was hit from behind on lap 61 and spun out. He finished all 74 laps but was twentieth. (Nigel Kinrade)

going into turn one. I was running real mean right there at the end. I passed Earnhardt with three laps to go and won the race."

Earnhardt dominated the points in 1994, but Rusty posted seven straight top-ten finishes, including three wins, down the stretch. He was second, 208 points behind Earnhardt, with four races to go. That's as far as he got. Rusty finished thirty-seventh, thirty-fifth, seventeenth, and thirty-second in the final four races. He dropped to third in points. The setback came as Parrott made plans to leave Penske South to become vice president of operations at Diamond Ridge Racing.

Still, with eight victories, Rusty had much to celebrate. He was the driving force behind Ford's victory in the manufacturer's championship. He had led 2,142 laps—more than 1 of every 5 laps run. And he had won eighteen races in two years—almost twice as many as any other driver.

With the 1995 season came a new crew chief, Robin Pemberton. But Rusty had a slow start, with two DNFs (did not finish) and other hard-luck races.

"We get along really great," says Pemberton, who celebrated his fifth anniversary with the team in 1999. "It's like any relationship. And some of your best relationships don't always start off the smoothest."

"It took about three-quarters of a year for us to meld," Pemberton says. "As different as our personalities seem to be, with him high strung and me laid back, there are parts of us that are pretty much the same. We're both slow to change on different things. But as we've grown together, we've become more alike in a lot of respects, such as our approach to cars."

With nine races left in 1995, Rusty caught fire again. He won at Richmond and had seven other top fives. He climbed to fifth in points. And as usual, he dominated the short tracks. He finished first and third at Richmond, first and third at Martinsville, second and fourth at North Wilkesboro, and second in the April race at Bristol. And the only reason he stumbled at the second Bristol race in August, where he finished twenty-first, was because Earnhardt turned him. Only 32 laps into the 500-lap race, Earnhardt tapped Rusty in the rear coming off the fourth turn, sending him into the frontstretch wall.

Earnhardt was particularly wild that night, even sending race winner Terry Labonte into a crash at the checkered flag. Rusty seethed as he limped around in a wrecked car, running only for points, watching Earnhardt wreak havoc. After the race, Rusty threw his water bottle at Earnhardt. It skipped off the

This sign, spotted at Pocono in 1994, is an example of the tremendous level of support Rusty's fans provide him. (Larry McTighe)

Rusty and crew chief Robin Pemberton watch a practice session from the roof of the team transporter before the Primestar 500 at Atlanta Motor Speedway in March 1997. "Rusty and Bobby Allison are probably the best I've been with in terms of working on their cars," Pemberton says. (Nigel Kinrade)

"Nowadays, you don't see drivers beating on each other. That's because if somebody hits one guy, the other guy is going to hit him back. In the old days, you'd hit them and knock them out of the way and go on."

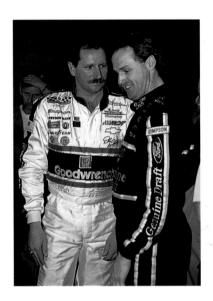

They've had their differences, but Rusty and Dale Earnhardt generally get along as well as any two drivers in the Winston Cup series. Rusty says Earnhardt without question is the toughest driver he's ever raced against. (Larry McTighe)

One week after their heated confrontation at Bristol, Rusty took a slight jab at Dale Earnhardt by placing this decal on the side of his car. (David Chobat)

roof of Earnhardt's car and hit him in the head. Rusty told him: "I ain't forgetting Talladega, and I'm not forgetting this!"

Rusty says today, "The only reason I threw the bottle was to get his attention. He wrecked me and he wrecked three or four other guys. And he ended up getting in the back of Labonte and wrecking him across the line. And everybody for some reason just thought it was the coolest thing in the world. He was down there smiling and telling his story, and I walked up to him and I wanted to talk to him. And I couldn't get his attention. So I took the bottle and slung it off his head, and then I got his attention.

"You can't take any crap off anybody. Nowadays, you don't see drivers beating on each other. That's because if somebody hits one guy, the other guy is going to hit him back. In the old days, you'd hit them and knock them out of the way and go on. But I think Dale and myself and all of us have learned that you can't do that anymore because everything is so competitive."

Earnhardt, Rusty says, is absolutely the toughest competitor he's ever raced against. "He always wants to be leading all the races," Rusty says. "He wants to get all the media attention. He just wants to be number one in everything he does. And I like to do that, too. I like the same exact thing. So we're very competitive when it comes to racing. Away from the racetrack, we get along really good. He'll be real talkative and a lot of fun. When he's on the racetrack, he's a brutal competitor."

The Earnhardt era ended with his seventh championship in 1994, and the Jeff Gordon era started. Gordon has dominated the series since winning his first championship in 1995.

Rusty, meanwhile, has struggled to achieve the consistency needed to win the championship. He finished seventh in points in 1996, with five victories but six DNFs. During the first half of the season, he flip-flopped between good races and bad races for four solid months. In between the bad races, he won about once a month from April through July. His victory at Pocono on July 21 was the forty-fifth of his career.

The year 1997 was even more of a struggle, with eleven DNFs, including five blown engines and four crashes. He won one race—at Richmond—and finished ninth in points. Part of the problem was that Pemberton

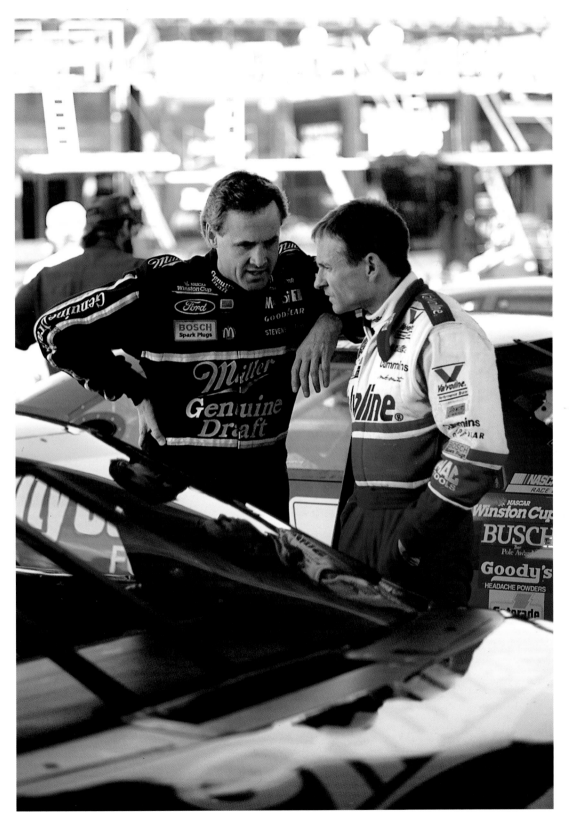

Rusty talks with Mark Martin before the 1994 Winston Select 500 at Talladega Superspeedway. "The thing that is amazing," Martin says, "is that we've raced against each other for twenty-two years and we've never been in a fight. And we've raced hard. A lot of those years we were fighting over the same turf—one little old prize in one little bitty pond—and we have never tangled. We have a lot of respect for each other." (Nigel Kinrade)

The 1998 season brought a new twist. For the first time in his Winston Cup career, Rusty had a teammate—Jeremy Mayfield—when Roger Penske bought a share of the car Mayfield drove. They hit it off well, and they seem to read their race cars the same. "He gets out of the car and I get in it, and our feelings seem to be identical," Rusty says. (Nigel Kinrade)

Opposite: Rusty's pit crew has always been known for its speed and efficiency. In this sequence, jackman Earl Barban and front-tire changer Billy Wilburn go to work as Rusty smokes to a halt in his pit at North Carolina Speedway during the 1997 AC Delco 400. (Nigel Kinrade)

and the team spent hundreds of hours developing the new Ford Taurus race car.

The Taurus debuted in 1998. And with it came a second Penske Winston Cup team. Penske became a partner in Michael Kranefuss's team. So Rusty started the year with a teammate, Jeremy Mayfield. The relationship clicked right from the start. Rusty won the Bud Shootout at Daytona—his first victory at Daytona—and started the year with five straight top-fives. He did not win a points race until Phoenix, but the victory kept alive his streak of winning at least one race a year since his first win in 1986—a span of thirteen seasons.

While Gordon has dominated of late, Rusty has been the only driver to really tangle with him on a regular basis. It started at Bristol in the spring of 1997. Rusty led 240 of the 500 laps, and was leading as the white flag fell. But Gordon tapped Rusty's rear bumper going into turn three, knocked him out of the groove, ducked under him, and sprinted ahead to win.

"The Bristol loss was a tough one," Rusty says. "That one bugged me because he ran into the back of me there and knocked me sideways. I don't like anybody running into me to pass me."

Rusty got a measure of revenge at Daytona in 1998 with his Bud Shootout victory. He gave the Taurus its first win when he jumped ahead of leader Gordon on the crucial final-lap restart, which was a double-file restart.

Gordon was so flustered by Rusty's move, he broke his transmission shifting into fourth gear while vainly trying to catch up. Rusty had listened carefully in the driver's meeting and knew where the cars were supposed to restart. "I wasn't going to sit there and wait for him to do what he had to do," Rusty said.

Rusty found himself behind Gordon at Richmond in June and showed no leniency. On lap 372, Gordon pulled outside Rusty and edged past going into turn one. As the two cars sped through turn two, Wallace's car washed up into the second lane. His right front fender caught Gordon's left rear. Gordon spun into the wall and was out of the race.

"A lot of people say that was payback at Richmond for the Bristol thing," Rusty says. "I'm not going to say it that way. I just think we got together at Richmond. But yes, I would drive in a little deeper for him, and I won't take any crap off him. I get along with him. I get along with all these drivers fine. I don't go to dinner with any of 'em. Maybe Earnhardt now and then. That's about it."

But Gordon came back on Rusty in the 1999 Daytona 500, making a breathtakingly dangerous three-wide pass for the lead with just ten laps to go. Gordon was below Wallace, on the apron, as they headed toward the first turn. Ricky Rudd's damaged car was already on the apron. To avoid a crash, Rusty moved up the track slightly to give Gordon the room he needed to get by Rudd. Gordon took it, passed Rusty, and won the race.

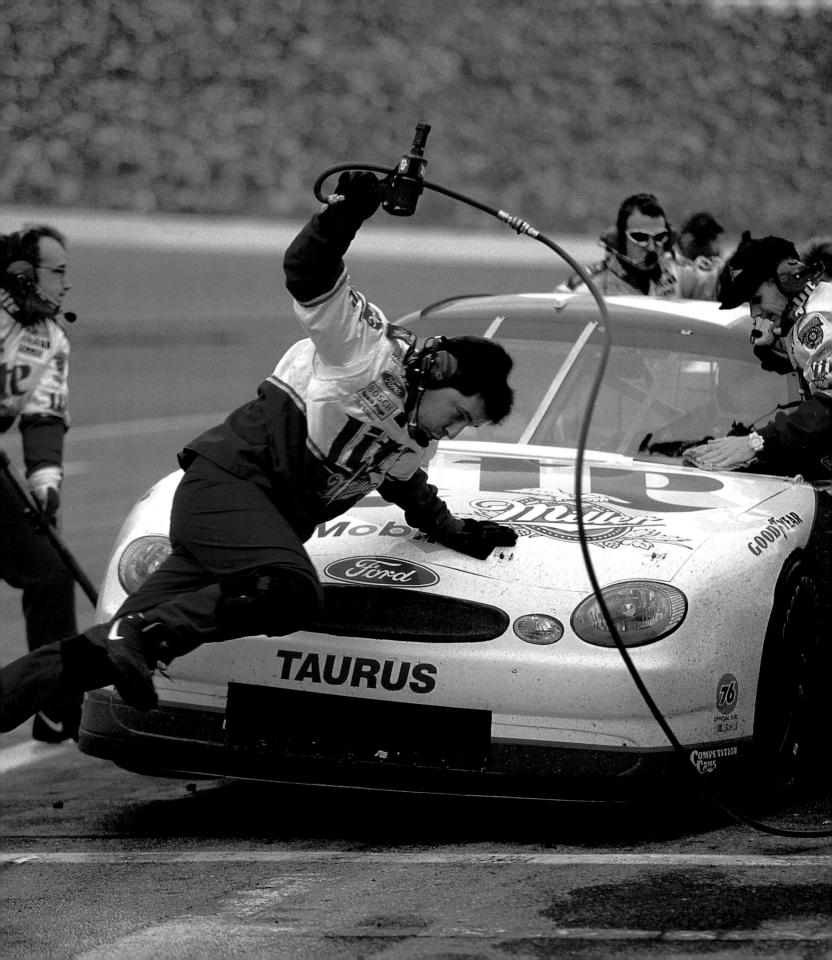

Lengthening shadows indicate the end of another long day at the track. Rusty (center) and his crew push the Miller Lite Ford Taurus down pit road at Texas Motor Speedway after qualifying for the inaugural running of the Texas 500 in 1997. Rusty's vocal criticism of the track surface helped lead to an extensive rebuilding before the 1999 season. (Lary McTighe)

"When the green flag drops, the bullshit stops. Rusty might have been in five different cities that week, but when he slips behind the wheel, he's the same racer he's always been. That fire is still in his eyes."

"If I hadn't moved, it would have been a real dangerous move on his part," Rusty says. "It may make me look like I was the quitter and I gave up. But I was at the point where I needed to do something. Because I was on the bottom and he was right underneath me. I don't think he would have been nuts enough to drive into the back of Ricky Rudd wide open. If I hadn't moved, maybe he would have jumped out of the gas real quick and tried to get back on the racetrack and got into my quarter panel in the process and maybe spun me out. That would have taken the whole field out. So I went up the track. He went right up with me. As soon as that happened, he got me.

"What would I do if I had it to do over again? I probably would stay right at the bottom of the racetrack and whatever happened, happened."

Rusty finished seventh in the 1999 Daytona 500. But it was his strongest run ever in NASCAR's biggest race. He led 104 laps. In his previous sixteen 500s, he had led a total of 17 laps.

These days, it is much tougher to win in the Winston Cup series. Every team works relentlessly for success. Nearly every team is making the sacrifices Rusty demanded of the Blue Max team after his decision to win in 1989.

"The competition is just so much tougher," Rusty says. "You look at Winston Cup qualifying, and everybody is bumper to bumper on the speed chart. You can run every lap and finish twenty-fifth or thirtieth. We think we're trying hard, but down deep I know there's probably some left. Unfortunately, the requests on my time—whether its from the media, the businesses I'm involved in, family, or whatever—the demands are greater right now than they ever have been. I'm doing more right now than I ever did in my life. It's easy for car owners and people to say, 'Hey, you need to get off that and pay more attention to the car.' But how do you do it? I'm the one who's supposed to take care of the sponsors and all that stuff."

The explosive growth of NASCAR has eliminated one worry that haunted Rusty most of his life—money. In addition to his income from racing, on and off the track, Rusty owns three car dealerships in Tennessee. In less than a decade, the Penske South shop has become too small. Lakeside Industrial Park, which had little racing presence before Penske South arrived, has become *the* place for NASCAR team shops. Up the street from Rusty's shop is the North Carolina Auto Racing Hall of Fame, another project Miller is closely tied to.

Rusty, meanwhile, has sunk several million dollars into his own lavish headquarters across the street. The home of Rusty Wallace Inc. is a place for all his associates and enterprises. He has a special autograph room where he can sign the hundreds of items sent by fans. In back, a big garage has enough room for his motor homes as well as his father's.

A puddle reflects Rusty's image with the trophy after his win in the rain-shortened race at Phoenix in 1998. The makeshift victory celebration took place at one end of the Dick Beaty Garage. "We targeted this race from the start," Rusty said. "It was a new car, new suspension, new motor, everything. We named it 'The Streaker' to keep my winning streak going." (Nigel Kinrade)

Family portraits from 1999 vacations show Rusty and Patti relaxing on a boat during their trip to the Bahamas, and their children, Greg, Stephen, and Katie, on the family's trip to the North Carolina Mountains. (Wallace collection)

Opposite: After many years of mostly heart-break at Daytona International Speedway, Rusty finally found victory circle when he snookered Jeff Gordon on the final restart of the 1988 Bud Shootout and pulled out to win. The win was particularly gratifying because it was the first actual race for Ford's new Taurus race car, which Rusty and his team developed. (Brian Cleary)

The blue-and-white Ford Tauruses of Rusty and Jeremy Mayfield roll past the front grandstand in the second running of the Texas 500 at Texas Motor Speedway in 1998. Mayfield won the pole but finished twenty-third. Rusty was twelfth. (Nigel Kinrade)

"This is a real important part of my life, and we're finally getting it all organized," he said during a visit in early 1999 as the building neared completion. As usual, Rusty was meticulous about every detail."

For years, Rusty's only love outside racing has been flying. "Bobby Allison got me into flying," Rusty says. "The first time I ever flew in a small airplane, there wasn't a cloud in the sky. It was beautiful. Oh, it turned me on. So I started flying in 1982, and I got my pilot's license in 1984. These days, Diamond Aviation consists of a Lear 31A private jet, a King Air 200, and a 407 Bell long-range helicopter. And they go all the time. The Lear hauls all of the team guys back and forth. The King Air brings the Sunday-only guys down. And the helicopter is transporting myself and VIPs all over the country. It's great for avoiding all this race traffic."

Russ and Judy moved to North Carolina in 1995. Until last year, Judy ran Rusty's fan club. Russ quit driving in the late 1970s. "I guess we go to twelve or fifteen a year," Russ says. "We've got a nice motor home, thanks to Rusty. But we can't hardly watch it on television no more. If he isn't leading, that's all right. But if he's leading, oh man! Can't watch."

"I used to never miss a lap," says Judy. "But it's gotten so bad, I put a tape in now. I go out shopping."

With almost thirty years of racing behind him, including sixteen in Winston Cup, Rusty can begin to see the end of his driving days. "I'll drive five more years," he says. "If I get tired and I get bored—if I get tired of the same old grind—then I'll quit. But I'm saying I'll drive at least five more years right now."

The transition may be natural. His youngest son, Stephen, twelve, has always loved racing and is currently racing Bandolero cars. "Even after I stop driving, I still plan on being very active with my team," Rusty says. "I have all the aspirations in the world for my son, Stephen, being my driver. All he's talking about now is race cars. All he wants to know about is shocks and springs and cam-shafts and ignition systems. He's doing all the same stuff I used to do."

"Times are changing," Miller says. "NASCAR is being invaded by big business, bigger sponsors, more politics. It gets crazy. But the more things change, the more they stay the same. When the green flag drops, the bullshit stops. Rusty might have been in five different cities that week, but when he slips behind the wheel, he's the same racer he's always been. That fire is still in his eyes. The team is strong. The cars and engines are great. For him, it's a long way from the end of the story."

The 700 horses under the hood of Rusty's Ford might need regular feeding, as suggested by the advertisement held by an autograph seeker at Pocono in 1994, but the appetites of autograph hounds are even more voracious. Here Rusty signs over the fence in the Pocono garage area. (Larry McTighe)